IT'S NOT SPECIAL

A Teacher's Journey in Special Education

Gene Thibeault

Gene Thibeault

Copyright © 2015 by Gene Thibeault

To my daughter, Woniya, and my wife, Deborah.
To my hard working parents Leo and Emma Thibeault
for a childhood that was all I could have wished for.
To my sisters, Sandy and Sally, who have always been
with me in times of need.
And most of all, to the many children whose lives have
touched mine throughout this story.

Gene Thibeault

THE QUITTER

By Gene Thibeault (with apologies to Robert Service)

When you're lost on the trail with the speed of a snail
And defeat looks you straight in the eye
And you're needing to sit, your whole being says quit
You're certain it's your time to die.
But the code of the trail is "Move forward, don't fail"
Though your knees and ego are scarred.
All the swelling and pain is just part of the game
In the long run it's quitting that's hard!

"I'm sick of the pain!" Well, now, that's a shame
But you're strong, you're healthy, and bright.
So you've had a bad stretch and you're ready to retch,
Shoulders back, move forward, and fight.
It's the plugging away that will win you the day,
Now don't be a loser my friend!
So the goal isn't near, why advance to the rear.
All struggles eventually end.

It's simple to cry that you're finished; and die.
It's easy to whimper and whine.
Move forward and fight, though there's no help in sight
You'll soon cross the lost finish line.
You'll come out of the black, with the wind at your back,
As the clouds start to part; there's the sun.
Then you'll know in your heart, as you did at the start.
You're not a quitter. You've won!!

TABLE OF CONTENTS

PREFACE

"In Utah we down climb, we don't need to burden ourselves with roping up when not necessary, not like those guys from California," said our experienced leader. I was a rookie at canyoneering and, at sixty-six, was neither as strong nor as flexible as I once was. The following morning I entered a slot canyon called Boss Hogg with trepidation. After a bone shaking four-wheel-drive ride, and an hour slog on slick rock and deep sand, we rappelled into the dark slot canyon. After an hour of easy down climbing, we came to an obstacle in the form of a ten foot drop. Our leader went first and easily found the hand and foot holds necessary to safely take him to the sandy bottom. My wife, Deborah, followed without incident as did Lila, a nurse who had canyoneering experience. I was next. I gripped a piece of webbing tied to a pack on the lip of the drop while the team leader held my left foot and instructed me to grasp a hand-hold to my right. To this day, I don't remember exactly what had occurred. I suddenly lost my grip, cartwheeled head-below-feet to the canyon floor, landing on a rib of sharp rock. Poof! The air was knocked from my lungs like a bellows emptying. I lay in the sand quietly for several seconds trying to regain my composure, then staggered to my feet only to feel an electric shock surge through my hip, back, and legs. I crumbled to the canyon's gritty bottom like a thrown sack of potatoes.

"Hon, are you all right?" Deborah asked.

"No," I grimaced. "I think I broke my hip." I tried once more to move, but the surge of pain returned with a vengeance. I could not move! Deborah and Lila tried to make me comfortable while the others decided who would go for help and who would stay. The good news—it was a warm day, a dry canyon, and only ten-thirty in the morning. The bad news—we were miles from anywhere. The nearest town was Hanksville, a small outpost high in the Southern Utah desert. Three members of our team began to up-climb the canyon backtracking toward our trailhead. This was no easy task, but they were experienced and eventually managed to find daylight, the trail, and the trucks. The others stayed in the canyon, Lila and Deborah with me and Dick, the trip leader, on top of the ledge. I knew I was in for a long day. If I did not move, the pain was tolerable, but sharp shocks pulsed deep into my hips whenever I flexed my legs. Minutes turned to hours, and I grew more and more introspective. I was sixty-six, had done everything I had wanted and more.

My mind returned to my time teaching disabled students. Thirty-two years of a career of rewards, successes, and failures. I felt that I had a story to tell and hoped that if I got out of this crease in the earth, I would tell my story, for my daughter if for no one else.

After six hours or more in the canyon we heard the thump, thump, of helicopter rotors. It was close, but we could not see it through the small opening above our heads. It passed once, twice, three times, then disappeared. An hour later it returned. I wondered aloud what good a helicopter was to me. They could not land near us, nor could a single chopper team provide a rescue. Still we wanted to be found, so we shined objects in the sun. The helicopter disappeared for a second time and was not heard again. By six in the evening we began to hear sounds in the upper reaches of the slot. Someone was down climbing toward us. We recognized the voice of Zig who was on our team. He was leading rescuers toward us. They seemed to be moving at a snail's pace. Over eight hours had passed since my fall, and help was now on the way. Finally, we heard a rope hit the canyon bottom and saw one of our team rappel beside me. He had a warm jacket for me and better still, news that an EMT team was only minutes behind. Soon a husband and wife EMT couple from Hanksville, Jessica and Duke, arrived on the scene and immediately began an assessment of my condition. I was given an IV, and my back was stabilized on a board. They were happy with my overall condition and emotional state, and assured me that a search and rescue team was on the way.

The shadows were deepening when we heard sounds coming from the canyon rim, voices called in an attempt to locate our position. Small stones were thrown down, and we gave directions until the rescue team was directly above. Jessica and Duke then had communication from the rescuers. Several more hours passed before we saw a rope descend from eighty feet above. Soon a rescuer, Steve, was lowered down the wall with a litter. He told the EMTs to prepare the "package"—me. I was given a shot of morphine after Jessica got permission from a doctor over her radio. A helicopter was called and would arrive shortly, *if* the winds allowed. Another half hour passed as they prepared me for the "lift." I was apprehensive about getting into the litter, but the experts handled me gently and the pain was less than anticipated. I was slowly hauled up the canyon by the high-angle rescue squad with a pulley system. Steve was lifted with me, kept the litter level, and talked me through the process. It had been twelve hours since the fall. On the edge of the canyon, I was blinded by lights and surprised by the number of volunteers. Thirty or more rescuers were involved in the operation. I thanked each of them as often as I could. They told me they enjoyed a rescue as opposed to a recovery. Soon we heard the thumping of a life flight helicopter. It could not land near the canyon lip safely, so I had to be carried several hundred yards up another sixty feet to a flat rocky bench. Within minutes, I was on board. Those with me in the slot were hauled to the canyon rim by the rescue team. Deborah gave me a quick kiss, told me she would see me in Provo, and I was flown from the crowd. A nurse practitioner, her assistant, the pilot, and I flew through a windy night toward the trauma hospital in Provo, a two hundred mile flight. In the hospital, I was treated immediately, given pain meds, and a CT scan. My hip was intact, but I had broken three transverse processes in my lumbar spine. Painful, indeed, but no surgery was necessary. I stayed two nights in the hospital, then Deborah and I headed south to St. George for rest and recuperation.

It has been over two years since my accident, and I am finally putting my fingers to keyboard. I began composing this memoir in the bottom of Boss Hogg canyon. It is about time I completed it. As I looked back on my teaching career, I hoped I have a story to tell. It is my story, my career, my thoughts and remembrances. How I chose this path, the changes I witnessed, and the people I met along the way are included. In my thirty-two years of teaching, Special Education has progressed from institutionalization of the "feeble-minded" to full inclusion of children with "special needs." I witnessed these changes first hand, for better or worse. Along the journey, I met wonderful and challenging students, fellow teachers, parents, and supervisors. I shared wonderful times and heartbreaks with friends and family. I have changed most of the names or used just first names in this tale. Indeed, I had difficulty with names, even when I taught. At sixty-nine, my mind is full of dents, but I have attempted to portray the events and times as they occurred. I included my childhood memories because they helped chart my course in life. My education and other normal human events, both positive and negative, shaped and molded my life and, therefore, my teaching. This also is the story of the many people I came to know in classrooms, on trails, and during good times and bad. They number over a thousand. The names may have been forgotten, but the events are still fresh in my mind. If I've made mistakes with dates and locations, I can only state that I did my best.

CHAPTER 1

DERRY

"There are only two things wrong with Special Education. One, it isn't special, and two, it isn't education." Did I just hear that correctly? These words were coming from the mouth and mind of my mentor, Dr. Lovering. What am I doing here during my second semester at Keene State College if that were true? I had the usual liberal notions that I was going to help those children who had been denied an education in their home schools, often their home towns. Was I wrong? Let's go back, way back.

I grew up in the small town of Derry in southeastern New Hampshire. It, like many New England towns of that era, was a factory town. In this case, three shoe factories dominated the landscape both physically and economically. My parents worked for the Kleve Brothers Shoe Company which specialized in cheap women's high heels. My father, Leo, was a sole trimmer and my mother, Emma, was a "fancy-stitcher," although I never knew what the "fancy" meant. I have two older sisters. Sandy, eight years older and, Sally, older by six years. I spent much of my time with neighbor friends my own age, riding my bike and playing in the vacant lot next to our home. We lived in a two-story former farm house near the center of town and were a typical family of the fifties era, Catholic and working class. Our home on High St. was built in the 19th century. For added income, my dad always rented the floor above us. We had milk delivered to our front door, the garbage was picked up in an old model-T truck, and an ice man delivered his frozen bundle to our upstairs renters.

School was the focus of my early years. First grade found me at the brand new Grinnell Elementary School. I enjoyed school but never really stood out in class, was generally shy, and would not volunteer willingly. I blossomed somewhat in the second grade and remember my teacher, Mrs. Garner, fondly. She was also known as "Bunny" to my family, who became friendly with this newest teacher in town. My school was about a mile and a half from home, and I was instructed by my father to take the bus each morning. On one fair weather spring day, I decided to ignore my father and walk to school. Both of my parents were at work, so who was to know? On the way, I took a short cut around a small dam between a poultry farm and Hoods Pond. While scrambling over the loose rocks of the dam, I lost control of my paper bag containing my lunch and milk money for the following week. It fell into the dirty brown water of Beaver Brook and disappeared. I walked the rest of the way to school in silent dread, trying to develop a reasonable and believable story. I had no lunch and no milk money, so some older kid must have taken it. Right? Wrong! My lie was a delicately balanced house of cards.

When Mrs. Gardner questioned me about the lost item, the story took on a life of its own. Instead of attempting to take care of the problem, as I hoped she would, I found myself repeating the story to the principal, Mr. Griffin. To my second grade mind, Mr. Griffin was a person that only the President and God spoke to. The stiff principal was very sympathetic to my tale and personally walked me over to the nearby Junior High to find the culprit who had stolen this poor second grader's lunch. Shit, I was in over my head in a whirlpool of lies. He walked me through several classes, and then into my sister Sally's classroom. Oh no, it just got worse. Obviously I could not identify the thief. There was none. The remainder of the school day was spent in silent terror, not talking or even looking anyone in the eye.

I took the bus home, like an obedient son, and awaited my parents return from work. I heard them entering the house, then my sister relating the story of my day to them. "Gene come down here now," my dad called. I took the long slow walk down my flight of stairs, like a "dead man walking." My entire family waited around the kitchen table. The grilling from my father didn't last long. I realized that confession, and taking my punishment, was the only sensible conclusion to this horrendous day. Crying, shaking, and hoping for mercy, I told the story, the truthful one this time. Looking back, my wise parents gave me the most appropriate penalty available, stay in my room for the weekend, extra chores to pay back the milk money, a full confession to the compassionate Mrs. Gardner, and then to the frightening principal, Mr. Griffin. Monday morning, I was ready to face the consequences. Mrs. Gardner had already heard from my parents on the phone. She told me to go down to the Principal's office and await my fate. I received only a lecture on honesty from Mr. Griffin and was told to return to class, take the bus from now on, and be careful of lies, because they have a life of their own. The lesson was well learned, and to this day I am a poor liar no matter how hard I try. I met Mr. Griffin some forty years later. He was a frail, small, old man. When I told him my second grader's story, his face lit up. "Oh, yes, I do recall that incident," he stated with a smile on his wrinkled face. "Did you learn your lesson?" he asked. Indeed I had.

In the third grade, I transferred to the brand new parish school, Saint Thomas Aquinas Elementary. The classes were small, the Sisters of Mercy were the not so merciful teachers, but best of all I could walk to school. I did enjoy my classmates, and that is a good thing, because we were together through the eighth grade. I was, at best, an average student never excelling, but not falling too far behind. Spelling, math, and penmanship were my banes as they are to this day. I loved reading, social studies, and recess. PE was usually a basketball and the neighbor's hoop. The school, of course, was next to the Catholic Church, and we had many visits from the parish priest. I became an altar boy during the fifth grade, and this allowed me some special privileges, best among them was leaving school to serve at funerals. Most of the nuns were strict and, dare I say it, "holier than thou." The exception was our seventh grade teacher, Sister Mary Eleanor. I met her the first day of my seventh school year and realized immediately that there was a kind, caring person under the starched habit. Math finally became a friend, my grades improved, and I joined the school basketball team. I grew faster than most of the other boys, and by eighth grade, along with shaving and a deep voice, was the center of the team. Our coach, Kans Beareau, was a wise, kind man, and not a bad coach to boot. We won some games but lost far more than our share. One winter's evening, we were invited to play a game at Boston Garden two hours before the Boston Celtics met the Detroit Pistons. We lost badly in the empty arena, but had front row seats for the Celtics game. My shinning athletic moment came when I caught an out-of-bounds ball. The referee gestured for me to throw it to him, as did Celtic star Bob Cousy. I, of course, threw my pass to the "Couse." Not fifteen minutes of fame, more like five seconds, but memorable none the less.

Our eighth grade teacher was the much feared Sister Mary Bonaventure, a nun of indeterminate age. She was not only our eighth grade instructor, but the Principal, and Mother Superior at the local convent. Luckily, she spent a fair amount of time out of the classroom with her principal duties. I can still hear her footsteps and the rattling of those rosary beads as she approached the classroom. The chatter would cease, and we would get to our work with our heads down or hands in our laps. I believe my math took a spin in the southerly direction under S. M. Bonaventure's tutelage.

One winter morning, I got back at the respected, but dreaded, principal. She called me aside from our paperwork in order to fit me for a new altar boy cassock. The nuns did routine work for the parish as well as teach. She flipped the cassock over my head and asked me to stick my arms through the sleeves. This I did, with too much gusto. Whack! I hit the reverend mother square in the jaw with a balled fist. One of my better punches, I must say. She was startled, so was I. She ran from class with a touch of blood leaking from her mustached mouth. The class was stunned. The girls were sure I was about to be struck from above with heavenly wrath, while the boys gave me a silent nod of approval. S.M. Bonaventure returned to class looking none the worse for wear. She never mentioned the accident.

School days flew by. Summers were spent on bikes, swimming in Hood's pond, and occasionally riding all the way to Beaver Lake. Winters meant shoveling the nearby ponds to play hockey, or watching basketball games, spring and fall were "mud" seasons. My classmates were looking forward to leaving Saint Thomas and joining the much larger classes at the Junior High, which was ironically called Hood Junior High. It was named after the prominent Hood family who had supplied most of the milk and ice cream to southeastern New Hampshire. The good sisters tried to implore my parents to save my soul and send me to Bishop Bradley High. It was the only Catholic high school in the area and was in the largest city in the state, Manchester. Luckily, my parents decided that I should follow my sisters, attend Hood Junior High, then Pinkerton Academy for three years of high school.

Pinkerton, or "the Academy," is a Derry intuition that opened in 1814. It is unique because the Academy is privately run, but all high school aged students in the neighboring towns attend. It has a formal curriculum, its own farm, maple trees, a chapel, and a headmaster. The local heroes to pre-Pinkerton students were the Academy football players. The poet Robert Frost taught at Pinkerton. He often used his experiences as a failed farmer for inspiration in his poems. I could certainly relate to "swinging from birches," "good fences making good neighbors," and a local stream known as "West Running Brook."

Hood JHS was bewildering at first. No longer did I have the same twenty-eight classmates, but was overwhelmed by moving from home room to various classrooms. One teacher really inspired me. Mr. York taught Freshman English. He pounded English into us with sentence diagraming, composition, poetry, classic novels, and drama. I worked on the production of "Annie Get Your Gun" under his direction and was left with a lifelong love of musical theater. I remember him calling me out during one class. "Mr. Thibeault, you are blending into the far wall. Sit up front where you can't hide." Thank you, Mr. York.

I was fortunate to make the Hood basketball team as a starter. By this time my classmates' growth caught up to my early spurt. I was now a forward, and a small one at that. Once settled into this new environment, I began to really enjoy school especially science, history and, for the first time, formal P.E. The reconstruction of a cat skeleton for the annual science fair was a memorable experience. I'd found a recently run-over cat on the side of the road and thought, why not? My mother was not pleased with a cat boiling on her stove when she arrived home. I explained, "Mom, I am going to extract the flesh from the bones by boiling." I finished the job on the outdoor barbecue. Winning a blue ribbon at the science fair calmed my mother. I was shattered when a fellow student threw a book at a classmate. He missed his target, but not my science project. Mr. Settle, our science teacher, apologized and gave me a brown paper bag with cat bones. The cat was interred in a hall trash can along with my ego. I endured—the science project did not

The fall of that year, I had the privilege of attending an election eve speech by the presidential candidate, John F Kennedy. As the motorcade passed my friend and me, JFK and Robert Kennedy looked directly at us and waved. I have been a political enthusiast ever since. The highlight of the year came on May 5, 1961. We were called into our homerooms at Hood and watched grainy TVs as Derry's own Alan Shepard rode *Freedom 7* into a sub-orbital ride in space. We were released from school early, and within hours a parade was organized on Derry's main street. Marching bands from neighboring towns and thousands of people poured into our little town. Derry briefly became known as "Spacetown USA." It was a celebration never to be forgotten. The gala came exactly one year after a devastating fire leveled one of our shoe factories and several city blocks. It made the Shepard celebration especially poignant.

So it was on to Pinkerton Academy. I had much to live up to. Both sisters were accomplished students, and the majority of the teachers still remembered them fondly. Pinkerton's red brick main building sits on top of a hill in Derry Village. "The Village," closely resembles the stereotypical New England town, unlike the factory town of Derry. It has the requisite white church on the hill and the white clapboard homes surrounded by huge maples. Pinkerton is steep in tradition. The front steps of the main building were for seniors only, and the original building, built in 1814, was still in use.

Instead of academics, I relished playing football for the "Red and White." As a sophomore (we had no freshmen), we were used as tackling dummies by the upperclassmen. We labored through the multiple bruising and insults but were rewarded by playing in junior varsity games. I was chosen as an end. That made little sense, because I could not wear my glasses while playing, thus actually catching a ball was an act of faith. I fondly remember my good friend and QB, Bruce, calling a "49 Charlie Deep" against the rival Manchester West. That was a play for me, if all went well. Somehow out of the eye fog my hands found the leather ball, and I was alone in the end zone. "TD Thibeault?" Not quite. Later that season I was called to dress for an away varsity game at powerful Exeter. My friends, who were not so blessed, chided me as I lay on a bench with cotton stuffed up my bleeding nose as the Star Spangled Banner began to play. Once again, I was relegated to tackling dummy status in pre-game warm-ups and thus suffered my first football injury. The last game of the year was against the hated and feared Somersworth High. Coach Wes Root called me aside early in the week before the game. "Thibeault, D. White is hurt and I need you to start Saturday at defensive end." Great! Wait! Somersworth runs a single wing which means the entire backfield and several linemen will attempt to rumble around the corner. I would be *that* corner. Coach Root gave me rib protectors and told me just take down as many men as I could, "Let our linebackers and DBs do the tackling." My poor eyesight perhaps was a benefit. I was bruised, battered, and as happy as a 155 pound defensive end could be. In my junior and senior years, I continued to play football. As was the norm for small schools, I played offense, defensive, and special teams. "TD Thibeault" didn't reappear until a wet Saturday when I missed a block, causing our halfback to fumble into the end zone. I jumped on the ball for the touchdown but caught the ire of the coach, not to mention the halfback, for the missed block. We had our highs and lows as a team. Our shining moment came once again against the league leading powerhouse Somersworth. It was the last game of the season and we were huge underdogs. Battle as we might, we failed to score for three quarters, yet our defense was strong. We were trailing six to nothing as time melted away. We drove to the twenty yard line when my number was called on a bootleg. My vision had not improved but was strong enough to throw a block and allow our quarterback to stroll into pay dirt untouched. Our extra point was good. Eight to Six PA! Derry, like most small towns, was proud of their team and I was proud to be a part of it. My dad and brother-in-law, Jack, attended every game, home and away. That meant a great deal to me.

At PA I loved biology above all other classes. Mr. Root, our football coach, was the instructor. Strange as he was, I learned a great deal, he sparked my imagination, and I developed a lifelong love of science. I soon found a social group where I could fit in. Sports was my outlet, instead of pursuing girls. I was still shy, although I did manage to attend the junior and senior proms. I tried out for the school basketball team. At five foot nine, I was no longer a forward and was not skilled as a guard. Instead I spent the winters playing for the local Catholic Youth Organization (CYO) team as a reluctant point guard. It was fun, but we were badly out classed against teams from neighboring Lawrence, Mass. In the spring, I tried out for the PA track team. This, I could do. I may have been too small at defensive end, and too short for varsity basketball, but I could fly around our dirt track at the half mile, quarter mile, and the mile relay. I won my share of races and in my senior year was named track captain. I made it to the state track meet that year, finishing a strong sixth in the quarter mile.

My senior year was whizzing by, and the reality of leaving PA took hold. My classmates and I shared three wonderful years, experiencing corn roasts, trips to the coast, pep rallies, and all the games. However, the terror of JFK's murder and the start of the Vietnam War broke our sense of isolation.

I had taken some courses in art thinking that I had some potential. I was, after all, the PA class artist. Well, the truth of the matter struck me like a slow fused grenade. I was not talented enough to actually pursue a career in art. Not many are. It was for enjoyment, not employment. I had worked two summers in the shoe factories and knew that I did not want to end up there. I will always be grateful to my parents for showing me the "joys" of laboring in a factory eight hours a day. I applied to two state colleges, Plymouth and Keene. Both my sisters attended Plymouth, but I opted for Keene, not having any set direction, I just needed to get out of Dodge.

CHAPTER 2
KEENE STATE

Leaving my home in Derry for the first time was not problematic. Keene was familiar to me. My mother was born there, and my parents were married at the local Catholic Church. Although, as a youngster I dreaded the two hour ride on State 101 through small towns, over hills, and around Mount Monadnock to visit relatives; (car sick and bored), I was happy to be on my own and looking forward to actually studying. Mom and Dad valued education and scraped enough money together to get me started. My summer wages at the shoe factory and some student loans provided the rest. I knew I would have to find some work in Keene as well as summer employment if I was to stay the four years it would take to graduate.

Keene State was a small college with an enrollment of about fifteen-hundred full time students. Education majors were in the majority, indeed the school was once Keene Normal School. Along with its sister college at Plymouth, Keene provided the majority of teachers in New Hampshire public schools. I had several friends from PA who were joining me at Keene. I chose a friend as my dorm-mate, but that lasted only one semester. He became the freshman class president. With his new celebrity and his annoying clock, I searched for a more comfortable environment.

I started my freshman classes in the general education curriculum. Elementary education seemed a good fit for me, and it was not because the females outnumbered the males five or six to one. Although that was a nice bonus. I found the work challenging but also stimulating. I was not a great student throughout grade school but managed to improve as the years went by and I gained maturity. I seemed to flourish in college, perhaps because I was actually paying for the privilege or because there was an expectation of a career in a few short years. I guess I had a focus for the first time.

I discovered that there was a Special Education curriculum available. It intrigued me even more than elementary ed., and I enrolled in the program my second semester. The classes were small and the instructors personable. Yes, I said to myself, this is what I want to do.

A notable field trip during my second year laid the foundation for my new career. A visiting professor, Doctor Gomes, had worked for the state of Massachusetts developing Special Education curricula. He took our small class aboard a school van, and we headed south to Fernald State School in Waltham, Mass. The "school" was huge, consisting of seventy-two buildings on one hundred sixty-eight acres. What I saw was shocking. The dorms had thirty or more beds, many containing children of six or seven years of age in diapers, some self-stimming by banging their heads, or twirling their hands in never ending games of self-discovery. Many of the older residents wandered day-rooms bare-footed while drooling in sodden hospital gowns. The majority of the staff, though caring, were nothing more than over worked, underpaid guardians. This was not special, and it certainly was not education. The majority of the residents were children who were taken from their homes and "institutionalized," often at birth by well-meaning, but short-sighted, doctors or other "care" givers. I saw this as a waste of lives and potential. Agreeably these individuals were moderately to severely impaired, but didn't they have the right to lead comfortable lives with worth? Shouldn't our society provide a more stimulating environment and meaningful existence for its less capable citizens? I had just witnessed a hell on earth.

Dr. Gomes introduced a book entitled "Christmas in Purgatory" by Blatt and Kaplan. It was a photographic essay detailing the horrid conditions in four eastern state schools for the "Mentally Retarded." It was a grim document. The photos were in grainy black and white and shot secretly. The conditions were reminiscent of WWII prison camps. Naked individuals, broken toilets, and hopeless misery. There was no chance of escape, no dignity, and very little stimulation in their lives. The general public, if they cared to look, could see what these poor souls suffered on a daily bases. As Miguel de Cervantes once said, they could no longer "cover a dung hill with a piece of tapestry when a procession goes by." Robert Kennedy and Nelson Rockefeller became engaged in the fight for these forgotten citizens. Our visit and this book provided me with a life goal of trying to put some special and education back into the mainstream. I now wanted a Special Education major.

During my sophomore year, I felt very comfortable at Keene State. I seldom returned to Derry during the weekends for care and comfort but did so occasionally to keep my parents happy and get laundry done correctly. I joined one of the three fraternities on Campus, had a painful romantic breakup, and pushed forward with studies. My grades were in the B-plus range, and I took all the Special Ed. courses that were offered. A major setback suddenly loomed. Special Ed. as a major was no longer available, so I would have to pursue a B.ED in elementary education with a Special Education emphasis. I would have enough Special Ed. coursework to earn a teaching credential in the field, but many courses from the school catalog were no longer offered. I joined the Student Council for Exceptional Children (SCEC). It was the student section of the national council. I attended several conferences that included professors, parents, and other professionals in the field. At one of these, Dr. Lovering introduced me to Manhattans. I was truly in the right field.

The time flew by and during the spring semester of my sophomore year I was able to find housing at the Alpha Fraternity. My roommate was a tall Vermonter nicknamed "Lurch" after the likable character in the "Adams Family." Phil aka "Lurch" was a Special Ed. student as well and we became close friends. We visited each other's homes and traveled to New York City and Montreal together. We were often called Mutt and Jeff by our fraternity brothers. He at six feet four, and me pushing five nine. I discovered in later years he became the director of Special Services in Lancaster County, Pennsylvania. I wonder if they call him "Dr. Lurch," but I digress.

In the spring of my sophomore year, I became friendly with a senior named Tom Duggan. He was the president of the SCEC. Tom grew up in the small central NH town of Hillsboro with his dad who was the caretaker of a very special boy's camp. Camp Wediko was founded by Dr. Robert Young, a PHD from Harvard, as a summer program for boys with emotional difficulties. The campers could go to summer camp and enjoy all the "normal" activities but also get the psychological counseling they needed and the fun they deserved. Tom not only grew up working summers at the camp, but became the head counselor while still in college. Tom thought that I would fit in with the camp staff because of my interest in Special Ed. and my New Hampshire upbringing. He said too many of the summer staff were city raised, city educated, and not at home in the woods. He offered me a position as the outdoor skills counselor. I gladly accepted. The position was not going to pay well, but the experience would be invaluable, plus I wouldn't be spending any money.

When I met the other staff during camp's first week, I was immediately impressed and apprehensive. Most came from Harvard and other elite schools. On the clinical staff was a PHD from Michigan State, a doctor Kempler. He brought several of his top students with him. Soon, however, I found that readying the camp by refloating the dock or sweeping spiders from the cabins didn't take an Ivy League education.

The following week the buses rolled down the long dirt road to Black Pond and unloaded a troop of anxious boys. After cabin assignments, unpacking, and a quick lunch in the mess hall, we marched the boys in a long procession through camp and down a wooded road with steep hills that dead-ended after two miles. All counselors were covered in mosquito repellant of the strongest kind, the campers were not. This annual hike had a purpose. If a camper were to become a "runner," he would likely head toward town on the six mile gravel road and hopefully would soon be discovered and returned to Wediko. Camp lasted six weeks and only one boy got beyond the six mile road. He, unbelievably, was found hitching on the Mass Turnpike, within sight of the Boston Skyline.

There were some seventy campers, all boys, ranging in age from seven to fourteen. Our camper to staff ratio was about three to one, much higher than in traditional summer programs. Most of the boys came from the greater Boston area, but a handful were from Harlem, NY. Our campers were totally unaccustomed to living in the woods, but most soon adapted. To the casual observer the camp would seem like any other, boys swimming in the lake, working on arts and crafts, or enjoying camp fires. The staff, comprised mostly of college students with an interest in abnormal psychology or Special Ed., took on the roles of traditional camping counselors. We were, however, providing psychological support as well. The clinical and nursing staffs were older and were working professionals. Each member of the staff had to sit with one of the staff psychologists on a regular basis to work on our own mental health concerns. It was hard work as we were on call twenty-four-seven. We had no days off during the first and last weeks. When we did have an off day it was for twenty-four hours only, and most of that time was spent catching up on much needed rest. I worked as an activities instructor, part-time cabin counselor, and all around go-for.

We all had multifunctional rolls. Most of the boys settled in well in spite of the first week of "liquid sunshine." Anger management, bullying, home sickness, and impulse control issues were dealt with on a routine basis. We learned how to hold a child physically when he was out of control. When a boy was unmanageable, we held him from behind while crossing his arms in front of his chest. We would release one arm at a time when he was calmer and always talked him down in a non-threatening voice. I seldom used this technique, but it was effective if necessary. A session with clinical staff would follow anger outbursts for both counselor and camper.

One memorable night I shall never forget, Harry Parrad, a bright Harvard student and a showman, was acting as host during the intermission of our weekly film in the mess hall. Harry had on his Groucho Marx outfit, mustache, glasses and all. He was calling up campers to the stage and handing out a candy bar if they answered his simple questions correctly. Suddenly, our "Groucho" screamed, "You just said the magic word," and threw about two dozen Snickers bars into the audience. An all-out riot ensued. Fights broke out, campers ran for the woods to consume as many chocolate treats as possible before being rounded up, and counselors recovered from heavy fits of laughter to chase campers while trying to restore order. It was known as the night Wediko went "bull-luby." Not only did Harry recover, he is now Doctor Parrad, the director of Wediko Children's Services and a well-respected clinician.

Later that summer, a small fire broke out in the sports equipment shack. It was purposely lit and was quickly subdued by the staff. Still sports equipment was destroyed and a dangerous incident went unsolved, until an older camper began approaching the staff issuing statements like, "I know you are talking about me," or "I bet you think I started that fire." It soon became apparent that "He doth protest too much." His clinical counselor got the truth out of him and he became the only camper, up to that time, to be sent away from camp as a danger to himself and others. Years later while visiting my family, the local news flashed a picture of a twenty-year-old in handcuffs being led away by police. He had just been arrested for arson and subsequent manslaughter. You guessed it. That was our boy. Not every Wediko story was a success.

One particular and peculiar child was my camp favorite. Harold was a clumsy affable misfit. The staff found him engaging and innocent, but troubled. The campers found him a suitable target for abuse. Poor Harold would be egged on by some unscrupulous bunkmates and call out to me, "Hey Gene, f*ck you, Gene." He would then immediately feel guilt and beg my forgiveness. "I'm sorry Gene, I'm sorry." Camp life for Harold was challenging. We could not overly protect him but did watch out for his safety. One boy in particular was Harold's bane. He went way over the top and forced Harold to injure himself several times. These two had to be kept apart. On "parent day," the fathers of both boys got into a heated argument, and they had to be separated. The apple does indeed fall close to the tree.

One morning on the way to lunch, Harold was late as usual. He suddenly burst into the mess hall screaming that a boy was in trouble in the lake. Sure enough, a camper had fallen off the dock fully clothed and was struggling to stay afloat. One of the staff jumped in and pulled him out of the aptly-named Black Pond. Harold was treated as a hero for helping save the boy. On the last night of camp there was an awards dinner. Campers received ribbons for completing swimming classes, canoeing, archery or, starting a proper campfire. The biggest award on the biggest night of camp went to Harold for saving a life. The clinical, nursing, and counselor staff were in tears as the campers gave Harold a standing ovation. He beamed!

Camp was over in the blink of an eye. It was time to put away the docks, store the bunks till next summer, and eat pizza, and drink beer, lots of beer! One poor camper was being picked up late by his parents. As the buses rolled over the bridge and out of sight, the poor kid was shocked by our behavior. We were behavioral roll-models until the campers departed, then, "Bull-luby!" We were throwing each other in the lake, lighting up cigars, and occasionally mooning each other. The renowned Dr. Young observed this and said, "In my day a simple display of the genitals was sufficient."

Later that week, I agreed to lead six of the staff on a hike to summit Mt. Washington, the highest peak in the northeast. We loaded our packs with personal gear, then added our community gear, which was mostly food as we would spend the night in the Tip-Top House bunkroom. Harry Parrad's pack was already full, therefore we took pity on this skinny

Harvard boy and shared his load equally. I'd been to the summit many times and knew the trail and hardships well. We struggled to the 6,288 foot summit via the Tuckerman Ravine trail. The whining terminated as we dug out our dinner and were astonished to see Harry pull out a large fluffy light-weight pillow. Daggers were aimed at Harry all the way off the mountain. Maybe a Harvard Education was superior after all.

I returned to Camp Wediko for another few sessions, but would not duplicate the initial six weeks. It was my first hands-on experience with children with "special needs," and I wanted more.

Junior year at KSC was very busy. I was elected head of the SCEC and Secretary of the Alpha Fraternity. Along with these extra duties, I worked as a teacher assistant in a local elementary school, and had a full load of classes. I still did well with studies earning a B-plus average. The fraternity provided a decent social life. I dated, but there was nothing serious. The 1966-1967 was a year of turmoil in the country, Keene however, was somewhat isolated. Free love, hippy culture, black power, and the drug scene hadn't made its way to southwestern New Hampshire *yet.* The Vietnam War was generally supported by our students. Politics was always on the front pages in New Hampshire, when the first in the nation presidential primaries were held in February. I saw Richard Nixon speak, while sitting next to John Chancellor at the local high school, and stood next to Nelson Rockefeller on a street corner. However, politics were not as relevant at KSC as Greek week. The exception was Keene State politics.

Alpha House put on a yearly satirical play, The Alpha Opera. We mocked the college staff, town officials, and anyone else we could slam. I was one of the writers along with our frat president Bob "Booby" Baines. We performed two shows and the majority of the students, administration, and faculty attended opening night. Our new college President, Dr. Zorn, was not amused when we panned him for firing a much loved member of the faculty. My song to the tune of "This Could be the Start of Something Big" was switched to "You Just Got the Call from Mr. Big." This song, among others, did not go over well with the pompous new president. He called the Alpha opera team into his office, threatening to stop the show if we didn't make changes. So much for the "First Amendment" at KSC. We acquiesced reluctantly and removed the offending song.

This was not my only conflict with the haughty Dr. Zorn. Our Special Ed. curriculum was in jeopardy because several of the classes offered in the college catalogue were no longer available. Dr. Lovering, as head of the department, was fighting for the program, but his hands were tied. We signed petitions and wrote letters to the administration to no avail. One member of the SCEC sent a letter to the Governor's office complaining. A formal letter was returned declaring that all the classes in the school catalogue were available. They were not! As president of the SCEC, I felt it my responsibility to respond, therefore I sent a reply to the State Capitol. Within a week I received the retort from the Governor's office. He did not want to be bothered with this nonsense again and referred me to Dr. Zorn. Shit, not again! I was in line to receive a senior year scholarship given to students working with special needs children. I was president of the SCEC, had the second highest GPA in our program, and God knows I needed the funds to get through my senior year. Did I just lose the funding I was counting on?

The summer before my senior year I worked as a playground supervisor for the Community Action Program. I traveled to Manchester daily to supervise activities on a playground and in a small activity center. My duties included managing a community baseball team, supervising Friday night dances, repairing equipment, and directing daily playground activities, such as breaking up fights. Kovalas Park was in a predominately Greek neighborhood and was noted as one of the more hazardous areas in the largest city in the state. I did enjoy the work even though my younger cousin, Russell, was my immediate boss. I was able to live at home and thus save money for my senior year.

The summer raced by as I prepared for my last year. I arranged housing in a large apartment, sharing with four fraternity brothers. We had enough room for sleeping and meals, but our bathroom was down a public hallway. Not ideal, but who needed to shower? Lurch also shared the apartment but drew the small straw and had a room that was no more than a walk-in closet. I returned to Keene early, hoping to find work for the first semester and anticipating that precious senior scholarship was mine.

While walking on Main Street with my laundry bag slung over my shoulder the week before school began, who should I encounter but the College President, Roman Zorn. Trying to avoid eye contact didn't work. I mumbled, "Hello, sir." He looked at me, pointing a finger, and asked, "You, you are that Thibeault, aren't you? You are the one throwing a monkey wrench into my curriculum." I tried to explain why I felt the need to respond to the letter from the Governor's office as I did. He just walked off in a huff, not listening. Bye-bye scholarship! I was right, I did not receive the money I had been depending on. It was given instead to a local doctor's son, who had little financial need and a lower GPA. When I questioned Dr. Lovering, he said he and his staff recommended me for one of the two prizes, but the final decision went to, you guessed it, Dr. Zorn. Screwed! My parents came through with some additional funding, and that combined with my limited savings, a student loan, and a job pumping gas, saw me through the senior year.

I spent the first semester on campus and the second student teaching in two separate locations. Classes went well as I had mostly electives after having completed the required courses the first three years. Fall turned into winter when lo and behold I met a freshman coed, Janice. Her home was in Derry, but we had never met because she was a recent transplant from Colorado. She had worked for two years before beginning her freshman year. I invited Janice to our annual winter party in the notorious Alpha House Cellar. I purchased a bottle of vodka and a quart of OJ to make screwdrivers. Janice lived in the freshman dorm which was strictly regulated back in 1967. When I arrived to pick her up, I was dismayed to find she wasn't there. In fact, I was told she left for the weekend. What? I was stood up, and by a freshman. Oh, the humility! I walked angrily to the Alpha House, where the tradition was to tend bar if you had no date and so reluctantly, I stepped behind the bar. I mixed drinks for a friend and his date, made myself a drink, danced with someone else's date, made myself a drink, poured a beer for a brother, and made myself a drink. Get the picture? I do remember being carried upstairs to a vacant room in the Alpha House. It is said that I broke the Alpha record for dry heaves. I remember holding the bed in a desperate attempt to keep it from spinning only to land on the floor as the room continued its' spiral. I was not a binge drinker, nor was I a teetotaler, but this was a first for me. There was discussion of sending me to the hospital, but the brothers thought that would reflect badly on the fraternity. Rather, I should die than besmirch the Alpha reputation.

That Sunday, I staggered over to Janice's dorm still in a fog. She was there! I asked her to take a walk with me, a slow walk. She explained, in her most heartfelt voice, that she had missed curfew on Friday night and rather than get in trouble called in saying she had left for home for the weekend. Instead, she stayed at a friend's home in town and was unable to contact me. This was long before cell-phones, and with skepticism, I bought the story. She cried and begged forgiveness. With a pounding headache and a sour stomach, I caved in. We held hands and walked miles in gently falling snow. I was smitten by this blonde-haired freshman with the smoky voice and dimpled smile. Janice and I continued seeing each other that winter and, in keeping with Alpha tradition, I gave her my fraternity pin as the brothers sang "Let me call you sweetheart" in front of her dorm.

My father helped me purchase a little red VW beetle that I would need as I began my student teaching. Fortunately, I was able to split my student teaching between fourth grade and Special Ed. I continued to live in the multi-room apartment but would be teaching special children in Claremont, NH, a forty mile one way drive on twisting roads beside the Connecticut River.

As was typical during the Sixties, the Claremont Special Class was not in a public school but was held in an attic over the city library. This "classroom" smelled of old furniture and moldy books, hardly the atmosphere for the integration that developmentally delayed children need to enter society. Still, compared to Fernald and institutions of that ilk, this was progress. The children lived in their homes surrounded by loving families. My supervising teacher, Mrs. White, was a young wife, a mother, and a skilled sensitive teacher. The first week, I worked with individual children and observed from the back of the room. After that I assumed more and more responsibilities. I fondly remember Joan, a girl of about twelve who was very overweight and overmedicated. She was a city councilman's daughter. Joan would often go to dreamland snoring loudly for an hour or more in the middle of the day. Mrs. White would gently sprinkle a few drops of water in Joan's direction. Joan would suddenly revive, mumbling, "Mrs. White, I think it is raining." The small class of ten, had several children with Down syndrome, two with autistic like symptoms, and a few who were just in the lower range of functioning.

One Friday afternoon, I went down to the library in search of a film. It was the Friday reward for surviving another week for both the children and the teachers. The always helpful, but overly sympathetic, librarian located a film about cows. Claremont is in a dairy producing area, so I said, "Great." I marched upstairs and loaded the ancient film projector without prescreening the movie. Mrs. White and I choked as the title came up on the scratchy black and white 8mm film, "The Artificial Insemination of Dairy Cattle." Holy sh*t! The kids went home none the worse for wear, and the good natured Mrs. White laughed it off. I shudder to think of what may have happened in today's PC environment. The Special Ed. internship lasted six weeks. Mrs. White and my supervising professor seemed pleased with my performance. I received an A for my efforts.

I found my routine that semester very perplexing. I would dress in a sports coat and tie; drive to "work," then return to life as a college student. The frantic mood in the country finally found its way onto our quite campus. The Vietnam War was raging and too many former classmates were now in uniform. Anyone who fell below a C average was invited to join the war effort. President Johnson chose not to run for a second term, Detroit was on fire, and Martin Luther King and Bobby Kennedy were on borrowed time.

A VISTA (Volunteers in Service to America) recruiter showed up on campus, and I filled out an application on a lark. The world was going crazy, why not find something equally bizarre. I thought no more about the VISTA program. Janice and I were inseparable even to the point of sharing time visiting each other's families for Sunday meals.

My second student teaching assignment was a fourth grade class in Keene. The school was in a turn-of-the-century brick building in the downtown area of the city. The supervising teacher was everything that Mrs. White was not. Mrs. Johnston, who was beyond middle aged, ran a strict classroom and seldom smiled. I was on my best behavior with only six weeks of college remaining. Once again I took a backseat for the first week while observing and taking notes. A former classmate of mine was on the faculty. It was his first assignment. He knowingly encouraged me to hang in there whenever we met in the lunchroom. Hang in I did. I found teaching fourth grade suited me. The children would pay attention to every word, were involved with their work, and genuinely yearned to learn. They seemed to enjoy my sense of humor after months of Mrs. Johnston's cheerless treatment. In April, I learned of the murder of Dr. King from another staff member while I had recess duty. I implored Mrs. Johnston to allow a student discussion on this horrendous news. Not to be. It was math time, then spelling. Let their parents deal with the current events. I held my tongue but felt hollow inside. It was a lost opportunity. Students should be able to discuss timely events. Should the classroom be so insular, that we could not even acknowledge news that will shape student's lives? My supervising professor, and even Mrs. Johnston, did admire my work (although she was not happy with my poor handwriting). I received another A for my second assignment. I had finally attained the elusive 4.0 for a semester.

I was chosen for recognition as a member of "Who's Who in American Colleges and Universities." Okay, so I had two brothers on the seven member committee, but hey? I interviewed for several teaching positions that spring and was offered a potential position in a small New Hampshire town as an elementary teacher. There were few Special Ed. assignments available. My future seemed secure. Teach, make some money, marry maybe, house, family, etc...

Then came the dreaded letter from my draft board. I was to report for a pre-induction physical one week after graduation; 1968 was the year when young college graduates were routinely drafted into the army or marines and immediately sent to Vietnam as second lieutenants. This was not how I had envisioned my career to evolve. I knew no one with influence to help me get the preferred positions of the army reserve, National Guard, Air Force, or the Navy. There was no way I would dodge the draft, so it looked like the military and Vietnam for me. A few weeks after that notable letter from Uncle Sam, another surprise letter arrived, a one page form letter. It sat on my bed while I joined some of my roommates for a beer or two. I opened the letter slowly and saw that it too came from the government. I'd almost forgotten about filling out an application for VISTA. My jaw dropped and I flopped on the bed. I was accepted into the program and would begin my training in San Francisco. I had never been west of Buffalo, NY. "Lurch, get in here. I'm going to San Francisco," I shouted. "No, you aren't, you're going to the Army," he laughed. I read the remainder of the letter. "Following training in San Francisco you will be assigned to the Oahu, Hawaii Program."

"You are shitting me," said Lurch. Wow! Now what? I had two weeks left of college life then graduation.

I returned to Derry to confront my parents with the news. My mother, of course, said, "You will take the teaching job." I tried to explain that teaching offers no exemption from the draft. She couldn't believe that the military would take her baby boy and ship him to the jungle in Southeast Asia. I knew better.

All that spring my stomach had been giving me fits. I went to our family doctor who suggested a test to see if the plumbing was malfunctioning. I had a hiatal hernia and inflamed stomach lining, probably the result of my record dry heaves. I mentioned to the doctor that I was due for my draft physical in a two weeks. He said that he would send me on my way with his report, but don't expect a pass.

At the urging of my brother-in-law, I made an appointment with the head of the local draft board. He was a former Army Officer with the unlikely name of Captain Gay (I kid you not). He said that *if* he met his quota, and *if* I was successful with the VISTA program, he *may* grant me a one year deferment. But, he cautioned, I would be number one on his list next year. Teaching would not get me off at all. Do I go directly to Vietnam or to Hawaii? Hmm, tough choice? Not! I called the Washington D.C office of VISTA and accepted their offer. I returned home and explained my decision to my parents. Understandably, it was tough for them to comprehend that I would not be earning money teaching in New Hampshire but instead would be five thousand miles from home surviving on a minimal living wage.

My parents, Janice, and I made the uncomfortable drive to the Keene State graduation. It was a somber celebration. Sadly Robert Kennedy was buried the same hour that I received my diploma. I said my goodbyes to classmates and teachers knowing we that may not be seeing each other again. The only light moment of the ceremony came when my fraternity brother, Winkey Basoukas, received his diploma. The big soft-hearted lug of a guy finally got into his cap and gown after six years of efforts. No one thought it could be done and he was given a standing ovation, even from Dr. Merrick who had failed him twice in basic biology. He would be a great teacher. I had two weeks at home before my physical and another two before heading to San Francisco for the VISTA program.

CHAPTER 3

HAWAII

On the day of the draft physical, I boarded a bus in Manchester along with thirty or more potential recruits. To my surprise, I knew a handful of my fellow draftees. Many were high school friends who had recently graduated, had dropped out of school, or had not maintained the highly prized C average. We drove through the early summer morning mist to Portsmouth in a bus filled with uneasy chatter. On arrival, we were greeted by a somber faced army officer and formed into lines as the role was called. The overall feeling was "You're in the army now." We filled out forms, were weighed, measured, poked, and prodded. My lucky friend Phil, stood six foot eight in his stocking feet. Military uniforms, bunks, seats, and the like, are not made for anyone more than six seven. Phil was stretching for all he was worth, while we silently cheered him on. During the vision check, Phil was measured, the dreaded butt check, he was measured, and so on down the line. After an immensely long morning of form filling, waiting in lines (no talking), and physical tests, we were called into a large room where a sergeant announced, "Does anyone have a reason why you cannot physically perform military duties?" At least half the hands went in the air, much to my despair. I was eventually called into a small chamber where a bored medic sat behind a metal desk. His attitude seemed to suggest, "My life sucks so yours is going to as well." He asked sarcastically, "What is your excuse?" I handed him my doctor's report about my hiatal hernia and inflamed stomach lining. He scoffed at it and sneered, "Not sure if Army or Marine food is best for that stomach soldier, but we sure as hell will find out. Back on the bench." It seemed that the next three years would not be my own. VISTA here I come, and then Uncle Sam would own me. The forty mile ride back to Manchester was subdued. Only tall Phil had a self-satisfied air about him.

The next few weeks were hectic. I had a frantic mother who thought I was running away from home, a girlfriend who promised to wait a year for my return, and a father who thought that I should have a real job that pays a real salary. I felt I had just dodged a bullet but knew that I only had one year before I might literally be dodging bullets. I bought new clothing that I assumed would be appropriate for Hawaii. I wasn't aware that New Hampshire department stores didn't know about Hawaii. Leaving Janice was gut wrenching. Although I had dated throughout college, ours was the only really serious relationship. There was no talk of marriage, but it was a real possibility. We saw each other daily and became fond of each other's families, mine of French Canadian heritage and Janice's Polish. Both families had strong Catholic backgrounds thus the parents approved. We escaped family pressure for a few days and went camping "up north," as they say in NH. My mother was in tears when I told her what we had done. "In the same tent?" she whimpered. If she only known what went on in college, her anguish would have increased tenfold. She, of course, thought her virgin son was soiled by spending two nights with his girlfriend. The truth is nothing occurred but snuggling and a few tears.

Eventually the day of reckoning arrived, and I drove with my parents to Logan Airport in Boston. In those days goodbyes were given at the departing gates. Mom and Dad waited until I headed down the ramp. Mom in tears, Dad consoling her, and me with a huge grin. I had only flown once in my life and that had been the short hop from New York to Boston after visiting Florida State University during spring break. Little did my parents know that a fraternity brother and I had delivered a car to a serviceman in Georgia, hitchhiked to Tallahassee then to New York, catching a flight to Boston, then a bus to Keene. I was looking forward to the great Wild West but had no clue of the path I was on. Strapping myself into my coach seat, I said hello to my seat partner. She was an eighty year old women dressed in Eastern European clothing. As we taxied she made the sign of the cross at least twenty times. During the six hour cross country flight, she said, "Yeah," only to the flight attendant.

"Would you care for a drink?"

"Yeah"

"Would you like a pillow?"

"Yeah"

I think you get the picture. Yeah?

My anxiety reached a peak as we touched down at SF International. I picked up my newly purchased luggage and caught a taxi heading to San Francisco State University for my two weeks of training. I was fascinated by the hills, lack of trees, brown color, and barrenness. Hey, there is the new stadium, Candlestick Park, and there is the Cow Palace. Fifteen dollars for a cab ride, you can't be serious!

SF State University in 1968 had quite a reputation. Its president, S.I. Haiakawa, had tried to squelch the free speech movement on campus only to have several administration buildings taken over by student and non-student protesters. Although this was the summer semester there was an underlying spirit of rebelliousness enveloping the campus. You're not at Keene State anymore.

I was assigned a room and a roomie, Bob. He was a shaggy-haired flower child from Northern California. I assumed he would give me pointers about life in San Francisco and hoped he would not think me a country bumpkin. Together we strolled into a conference room to meet our fellow trainees. The boys outnumbered the girls about three to one, perhaps the draft was responsible for this discrepancy. There were about twenty of us from various regions of the country.

"Hi, I'm Larry Wilson from West Virginia," insert Southern accent.

"I'm Dave from Minnesota," insert accent as in the Movie "Fargo."

"I'm Marcy from New York," insert Tony Soprano speak.

"I'm Gene from New Hamphsa," No accent heaah.

And so it went down the line. Regional accents aside, we were a pretty homogenous grouping, mostly white, well educated, and middle class. The VISTA regional director was a worn out bureaucrat who seemed to be counting the days till retirement. He spoke with all the lethargy of a sleeping dog.

On the other hand we had Buzz, who had two terms as a VISTA volunteer in Honolulu. He was a wealth of information. He knew and loved the island culture. We would be assigned as two or three person teams working in the poorer regions of Hawaii, mostly on Oahu, by far the most populous Island. It was not your tourist adventure. Among the Hawaiian wealth and the tourist meccas, there was a lower class living in poverty, predominantly native Hawaiians or Samoans.

In order to prepare us for the realities of the job, we would be given a stipend of fifteen dollars each and in teams of two and were asked to survive a full week in San Francisco. Ouch! My dorm-mate Bob and I teamed up. We did have transportation vouchers to bring us to and from the daily meetings, but little else. I was not aware that most of my fellow trainees carried one of Daddy's credit cards should they need extra help. Bob and I had no such fallback. On the first day of our poverty experiment, we headed into the squalid Mission District and found a rundown flop house. Our third floor room had only one double bed, a wash basin, and a shared bathroom down the hall. We had the remainder of the day to ourselves, and agreed to meet others in a local park for a free weekend concert. I was used to concerts in McGregor Park in Derry, with its small bandstand and picnics on blankets. I was unprepared for a concert in Golden Gate Park. The park is three miles long by half a mile wide. Derry could fit into this venue. After what seemed like miles of walking, we did find the concert. I thought I had heard everything, but this band, in my opinion, was dreadful. It featured a long-haired woman singer with a voice that had the tonal qualities of a garbage disposal.

"Who are these guys?" I asked all-knowing Bob.

"They're a local group, Janice Joplin with Big Brother and the Holding Company, or something like that."

"Hmm, they really suck," I replied.

We walked back past "Hippy Hill," around Keizer Stadium, and through Haight-Ashbury. We were constantly approached by unsavory characters offering illegal pharmaceuticals.

"Mary Jane? No? Hash then? No? I got LSD."

Wow, just like on TV.

Bob and I took the local transit back to our seedy room armed with a can of RAID like soldiers ready to battle invaders. As the door creaked open, my heart sank. Our luggage had been stolen! On reflection, I was incredibly naive to walk into this hardcore part of town dressed like a tourist carrying new luggage. Now what? Most everything I owned was in a closet in New Hampshire, all else was gone. Bob wisely had left most of his belongings in the dorm. We used a payphone and called Buzz. He said they had funds available for an emergency clothing allowance, and we should leave the fleabag hotel at once. It was a lesson learned. In America the poor are most often the victims of inner city crime.

Instead of returning to the dorm with our tails between our legs, we joined other volunteers who had found lodging in a housing project near Chinatown. We slept on the floor in a community recreation center, for free, no less. Now we had more cash for food so we did no dumpster diving. Dave, his partner Mike, and I became quite friendly whereas Bob, with whom I was teamed, was too over the edge for me. He washed out of the training program and never got to Hawaii.

We spent our days at the University being instructed in Hawaiian culture. We would be working exclusively in Hawaiian and Samoan neighborhoods. Only one assignment would not be on Oahu. A soon to be married couple from Minnesota were assigned a position on the Big Island of Hawaii. I was assigned a position on the Leeward Coast in the town of Nanakuli, partnering with two female volunteers, Lacy and Lorrie. Other groupings were spread around the Island. Dave and Mike were to be in a rough neighborhood near downtown Honolulu. Larry, from West Virginia, and his teammate were to be on the Windward Coast in Waimanalo, another pair managed the prime assignment on the North Coast where the big waves roll in from across the Pacific smashing surfers into the rocks at the Bonsai Pipeline. All of our housing would be Spartan at best, and our monthly stipend would barely cover expenses. Each team would be issued a government vehicle for transport and provided with health coverage. We would initially have hosts to help us orientate to the new surroundings and would be required to check in weekly with a supervisor, in our case, Buzz.

We dressed in our VISTA best and boarded Hawaiian Air for our five hour flight to Honolulu. The ancient bureaucrat, useless as usual, had to speak to us as a group just before takeoff. In his most dramatic voice he repeated the inspiring lyrics from the Man from LaMancha. "To dream the impossible dream," he began. I mean he spoke the entire song, as we all tried our best to hold back fits of laughter.

As our plan banked over Diamond Head then Waikiki, I felt like I was approaching another planet. Photos of Hawaii never revealed the crystal blue magic of the mid Pacific islands. We touched down on the humid tarmac, and as we descended the ramp the smell of tropical blossoms and the burning of sugar cane assaulted our senses. We said a quick goodbye to our friends, and were greeted by hosts from our assigned villages. "Alooohas," echoed through the halls. My partners, Lorrie and Lacy, were covered shoulders to ears in leis. I was draped in flowers as well. The three of us were whisked off to Nanakuli to receive even more leis and welcomes. It was entirely overwhelming and disquieting at the same time.

Entering the village of Nanakuli, I was surprised to see cacti as well as palm trees. The beach was long, the waves powerful, and the buildings modest. That day, in no special order, we met the Chief and the minister of the Samoan village, the head of the Community Action Program, the new school principal, and most of the elders in the Hawaiian Homesteads Community. I spent the first two weeks in the humble home of David Twig. He was the head of the local Community Action Program and the only federal agent in the community. I had a small room in his quonset hut. Nanakuli, although in a beautiful setting, is noted as being a no-go region for haoles (non-Pacific Islanders). Life was difficult here with crime, poverty, and poor school achievement. We joined the summer Community Action Program serving the children of the community, organizing recreational activities, helping with free lunches, and attending community meetings. After the summer program ended we would be asked to find a need that we could fill. Hopefully, in line with the community desires and our college training. In my case, I hoped to work with the local elementary school known as Nanaikapono. The Leeward Oahu School District had the lowest levels of school achievement in the entire state and Nanaikapono was at the bottom of the district. Attendance was low and parental support minimal.

Our first evening we were invited to attend a rehearsal of a pageant which was to take place in Honolulu at the end of summer. It would be a benefit to bring bus service to Nanakuli. Local children would be the singers and actors. The play was directed by a Mr. Boone, who was named as the formal head of the Mayor's council for Hawaiian Arts. It was thought he would be a figure-head only, but he jumped in and lent his considerable expertise to the production. Lorrie, Lacy, and I said, sure we would love to help out. We met in the local gym and were shocked to see that Mr. Boone was none other than Richard Boone, aka Paladin on TV and a renowned actor appearing in over fifty films. He shook hands with us and invited us to sit beside him. His famous booming voice would echo around the room as he instructed his actors, dancers, and singers in various aspects of the production. Upon the makeshift stage waltzed a nineteen-year-old Polynesian beauty. She embodied all the Hawaiian beauty clichés in one graceful package. Her name was Irma. She had that golden skin that James Michener had written about in his novel

"Hawaii." Mr. Boone poked me in the side saying, "I can make this young woman a star if I could convince her to return to Hollywood with me." It was obvious that he, too, was smitten with lovely Irma.

After the rehearsal, he invited us to head out to Makaha beach for a beer. You bet we said, and one of the most remarkable nights of my life continued. Makaha is a renowned surfing mecca. It was twenty miles west of Nanakuli. I sat on the beach with a beer watching a full moon fill the sky as the breakers were lit by luminescence. I had never been in warm ocean water and that alone was an unreal experience. Adding to the magic, Irma sat down beside me on a towel, her hair still wet from the sea. We made small talk and I realized that to her, I was as exotic as she was to me. The conversation came down to our hopes and dreams for the future. Reluctantly, I told her about Janice, maybe the military, and teaching in New Hampshire. She told me her wish was to become a Jehovah Witness Missionary, and how I could be saved if I accepted Jesus as my Lord and Savior. Wow, end of my fantasy, and Richard Boone's as well. The same night we met Al Kianoa, a burly long-haired lifeguard at Makaha. He would become a great friend and a mentor. He was quite fond of Lorrie, and I was welcome to tag-along.

We spent our first weeks becoming familiar with the Hawaiian and Samoan cultures, and they were as different from each other as mine was to theirs. Nanakuli was a Hawaiian Homestead village. Land had been deeded to native Hawaiians in trust when the Hawaii Islands were seeded to the US. There was no government official in the village, but a certain Mrs. Parker seemed to wield power. She was an older lady of considerable girth. If there was a conflict in the village, elders looked to her for guidance. I discovered she was a direct descendent of the Hawaiian royalty known as the Alii. We also learned about "island time." Meetings might be scheduled for seven pm, but don't expect a commencement until after eight. Directions were simple, Makua meant toward the mountains, Makai toward the sea, Eva toward the southern town of Eva, and Makaha toward the northern town of Makaha. On an island this made perfect sense.

The local Samoans had recently arrived from American Samoa and brought with them their set of values and traditions. We became welcome figures in the Samoan community. The chief was Fonoti and the minister Reverend Luto. They seem to have equal status in the village. We were invited to the chief's home for introductions. Although the humble home was fully furnished we sat on hand made mats on the floor. The chief would not acknowledge us until a "talking chief" introduced us to him formally. The introductions went something like this: "Chief, I would like you to meet Gene, he comes from far away New Hampshire as a volunteer to help the children of the village." When all the introductions were finished we were greeted with a hearty, "Talofa!" and invited to eat a meal with the men of the village. Although we had recently eaten, we felt that it would be poor manners not to accept. Bowls of fish, meat, rice, breadfruit, vegetables, and the ubiquitous poi, were placed in front of us. Once the chief had tasted, we dug in, but there was no way we could make a dent in this fare, even if we hadn't eaten in a month. Try we did. Lorrie looked at me as if to say, "I'm trying, but I can't have another bite." We didn't realize that this meal was meant to feed the women, children, and young men of the extended family after the honored guests took only the best portions, leaving the rest to be shared. A lesson in Samoan traditions learned. Another oddity was the concept of ownership. If an item is not being used, it is essentially community property. My roommate, Dave Twigg, was dating the minister's daughter much to the consternation of the younger Samoan men. Dave once laid his favorite pair of sunglasses on a bench when visiting Laalofi, his girlfriend. He saw his prized glasses pass by on a broad bodied young villager. He could say nothing. So it went in Samoa, and so it went in Nanakuli.

Our daily schedule revolved around the children's summer program. One of the directors was a cheerful strongly built young Samoan named Sui. He was a linebacker for the University of Missouri, but was a gentle and professional young man with a genuine smile. Toward the end of the summer we were stunned to find that he was diagnosed with Hanson's Disease, also known as leprosy. His football career was over. We visited him at the hospital, and he maintained his good spirits and sense of humor. He spent an entire year in quarantine from his village. He was inspirational to all of us.

At night we helped with the play, chaperoned volleyball games or dances, and attended community meetings. After receiving Hawaiian driver's licenses we were given a government vehicle. It was a bottom of the barrel Nash

Rambler, but it did provide the three of us needed transportation. The girls found housing in a home at the far end of town right on the Farrington Highway. There was a small shack behind it, and the wily Chinese landlord agreed that I could stay there for a nominal fee. I moved in and set up home. In Nanakuli I only had to say I lived behind the two-story white house and any villager could place the home. I loved sleeping to the sound of the surf crashing on rocks across the highway.

We met often with the other volunteers, usually in Honolulu but occasionally at a picnic on a lovely stretch of beach. We did get a reprimand when a serviceman found four GSA vehicles parked at Pounders Beach with "for official use only" painted on the doors. Oops! We learned to be more discreet.

In early July, all volunteers were invited to a wedding on the big island of Hawaii. The VISTA couple from Minnesota were to be married in the native Hawaiian village of Milolii. They planned to wed before leaving for training but decided that a Hawaiian ceremony would be more meaningful. They were assigned as guardians of the village children during the school week because Milolii was thirty-five miles on a single lane road from the school in Kona. The children were bused to school on Monday mornings and returned home on Friday afternoons. Think about newlyweds parenting twenty children. We spent our first paychecks on the flight and car rentals, but it was well worth it.

On a Friday evening our eighteen-passenger prop plane landed at Kona. The wedding was Saturday. In order to save money, we made our way to Kealakekua Beach to spend the night sleeping on the sand. There were twelve of us in two rental cars. Crowed? You bet, but inexpensive. We bought snacks, drank Primo beer, and bedded down on a beautiful stretch of white sand. Within an hour, locals found our site and were ready to take us on. "We heard there were hippies on our beach and we no like stink-head hippies," the biggest of them said. We assured them of our good intentions and passed around Primo. Our attackers soon became our new friends. They spent the night "protecting" us from other islanders with more hostile intentions. We slept fitfully to the sound of guitars, laughter, and the pounding surf.

We hit the main road in the morning. After leaving the highway, we followed a dirt road to our destination. Milolii is a small village which sits between two volcanic flows. It had about two-hundred inhabitants, all of Hawaiian extraction. We were asked to set up sleeping bags in the community center, and to help with the wedding celebration. An imu was dug and a whole pig was prepared for the famous kalua pua'a. Breadfruit, coconut, poi, and, of course, Primo was to be served. The wedding was beautiful. Families of the bride and groom, the entire village, and all the VISTA crowd attended. After the ceremony we danced the Hukilau with the village chief giving instructions. Then it was into the water for my first snorkeling experience. I had never seen such colorful fish and pristine coral. We slept soundly with Primo dreams.

In the morning we piled into our rental cars, said our alohas, and drove around the island in the opposite direction from our start. At each pullout, we jumped out of the cars yelling "ooh" and loaded back in, changing seats and drivers. By late afternoon, we returned to the airport for our flight to Honolulu and our faithful Nash Ramblers.

Back in Nanakuli, I became close friends with Lorrie in a platonic sense. She was trying to come to terms with the disappearance of her younger sister. Foul play was indicated. She was heartbroken, and I offered what solace I could. Her home was in Walnut Creek, California and mine in Derry, but we did share a bond. We both were homesick and needed a friend. Lacy and Lorrie were not operating with the same set of rules. Calling Lacy scattered would be a kindness, yet they managed to work through their difficulties. I wrote to Janice and my parents several times per week but received limited response due to the ineptitude of the Hawaiian postal system. Letters to my parents were all airy and cheerful with limited details. Those to Janice were more on the maudlin side. I did receive a package from home which was part of the VISTA service. It felt like Christmas, opening the huge box containing goodies, including a small record player, some favorite 45s, books, and an eight-by-ten photo of Janice autographed with love. Another big surprise arrived the following week. I received a telegram from home. My parents had opened a letter from my draft board. I received a 4-F designation. I was unfit for military duty. The letter from the well-meaning doctor apparently had paid off.

In August the community was abuzz. Nanaikapono Elementary School had lowest achievement levels of any school in the state and a special training session was ordered by the Leeward Oahu School District in conjunction with the

University of Hawaii. This was something for me to be involved in. I was trained in elementary and Special Education, a perfect fit. The administrators, staff, parents, and even the students, were brought together to brainstorm in an attempt to find a solution to the school's poor academic performance. A long-haired slick talking PHD from the University named Scotty McDonald was in charge of the training. He was a rabble rouser from the start. During a well-attended community meeting he asked, "What can we do? What do we need in our school to make a difference? What one thing is the most important for our students?" The overwhelming consensus was, we need a better student to teacher ratio. "How many more teachers will make a significant difference?" Scotty asked. A very powerful community organizer said, "We need twice as many teachers."

"Well," said Scotty, "let's get them." Wow, I was impressed but very skeptical.

The very next week, the Leeward Oahu Schools personnel manager was asked to attend another community meeting. He said he couldn't provide any more staff for Nanikapono. "Who can?" asked an angry Polynesian crowd and, believe me, angry Hawaiians and Samoans are a group to be reckoned with. The next day another meeting was called and the Superintendent of the District was before an even larger crowd. "I cannot give you any more teachers without taking them from other schools," he stated. Just then the heat or tension got to him and he nearly passed out. A kindly and tactful Catholic nun who worked with the school took care of him. Within two days the Superintendent of the State Department of Education was in Nanakuli in front of an overflowing crowd of concerned community leaders, teachers, students, parents, and the media. His name was Ralph Kiyosaki. He stood about six-foot-six and his voice boomed off the auditorium walls. He quieted the crowed until he made a tactical error. He said, "I can change teachers into pencils and pencils into teachers." Boom, the crowd screamed, "teachers are not pencils or desks, or paper, we need teachers! How many can you give us?" He blinked twice and said, "I'll give you half of what you asked for this year and more if you are successful, but where will you house them?"

"I'll build a classroom in my garage," said one powerful mother. Scotty McDonald said, "We have a couple of weeks to work this out."

"I'll get you the teachers, you provide the funds." Polynesians are the most emotional people I have ever met. There was cheering, crying, and shouts of joyous laughter. Headlines in the Honolulu morning papers and the TV news proclaimed that Kiyosaki had gone overboard in offering one school some fifteen new teachers while other schools went begging. I was personally called into the home of the State Director of the Hawaiian Homesteads to relate my interpretation of the events. He asked me to keep him up to date on actions in Nanakuli.

In the meantime, I was hatching an idea. I had a new teaching degree and Nanaikapono was desperately trying to find teachers. If I could land a job at Nanaikapono, I would still be serving the community, in fact, helping more by being in the classroom. Janice could come to Hawaii and attend the U of H. We would have an income, though minimal as a beginning teacher. I spoke to the first year principal, Fred Cachola, and he agreed to hire me if my papers were in order, and he would rush me through the teacher credential paperwork. I also spoke to Buzz, my VISTA supervisor. His response was positive as well. He felt that service was service, and though he would miss me as a volunteer, he would welcome me as a member of the community. Now there was Janice. I wrote a carefully worded special airmail letter asking her to join me in Hawaii. Although I didn't say it outright, the implication was that we could be married if it all worked out. Within a week I received an airmail answer from her. She said YES!

I started the ball rolling and soon had my first teaching job, a second grade assignment. It was unheard of to have a male teacher in a Hawaiian second grade, but I relished the opportunity. I was to work with two other second grade teachers in what was called a three-on-two program, three teachers to two classrooms, thus solving the classroom space issue. This would bring the teacher pupil ratio from thirty to twenty to one. We still had a week of orientation and prep before school began. I would not have my own classroom but would have duties in both rooms, including working with any disabled children. I saw my role as a unique opportunity to work with a new culture in an exploratory program and although not Special Ed., it certainly involved children with unique needs.

I enrolled in a U of Hawaii educational psychology class taught by Scotty McDonald. He allowed me to write a paper on integrating physical education with the reading curriculum in lieu of attending weekly classes at the U of H. While reading was being taught, I took half the class for twenty minutes of outdoor physical activity. My kids would then be dismissed and switch with those in the classroom. I would do this with the two classes on alternate days. In other lessons, I would teach half a class in the rear of the room while the other teacher worked the front. My two partners were as different as pineapple and poi. Elaine was young, liberal, and kindly. Mrs. Cameron was in her late fifties, uptight, and domineering. Elaine's husband was serving in Vietnam and, like a number of teachers, she came from the mainland to be nearer to him. Mrs. Cameron was also married to a serviceman, but he was an officer stationed in Honolulu. In spite of their differences I was committed to work with both on an equal basis.

Just after Labor Day was my first day of school and, although I didn't realize it, it was the first day of a thirty-two year career. The first morning, I was on the playground dodging volleyballs and answering questions. The younger children asked, "Who are you?" "You gonna be my teacher?" The older kids were more standoffish and just glared as if to say, "You can't say nothing to me." The second graders were bright-eyed with gleaming dark faces and were excited to be back at school with friends.

I introduced myself to the students in Elaine's classroom first. They just couldn't get their tongues around Mr.

Thibeault and having met some of them during the summer program, I became simply Mr. Gene. Usually pronounced "Meesta Genes." I was fine with that, as was Elaine, Mrs. Cameron was not. She thought that it was disrespectful and that children in Hawaii should speak, dress, and act just as students do on the Mainland. There would be a continual disagreement between us. Shoes, for instance, were seldom worn by these island kids in their homes or on the street, but in Mrs. Cameron's class shoes were ALWAYS worn. Elaine was more forgiving and would allow her students to put their shoes under desks while working.

Second grade is one of my favorite assignments. The children have been socialized, tend to be orderly, and while they can be silly and loud, they hang on your every word. Now I am generalizing. My students were almost all of Hawaiian extraction the only exceptions were those from the Samoan village. One small imp of a boy was Tomato; pronounced the British way with the long "a" sound. He was very shy and would love to melt into the background if one would allow it. In class, I would assist him with math and be rewarded with a white-toothed grin that could light up a dark cellar. He was a slow and reluctant learner. As with most of the Samoan children, he was born in American Samoa and had to adapt to a new culture when away from his neighborhood. There were many altercations between the native Hawaiians and the Samoans, but seldom among the lower grades and never in my classes.

Nanaikapono Elementary School was built as a series of long single story buildings with screens and shutters but no glass windows. Because it was situated on the ocean side of the Farrington Highway, the sound of the surf was always in the background. I found it refreshing and soothing most of the time. However, when the storm waves rolled in across the Pacific, they were thunderous and a real distraction in the class. Sometimes, I could see the crests of the breakers rising and falling through the screened windows. At recess we had to enforce a no-go zone near the coral rocks that separated the classrooms from the sea.

I had a real soft spot for my second grade girls. Their thin, brown legs would stick out from brightly-colored loose fitting dresses. Wild hair with plumeria blossoms, and shining dark eyes greeted me each morning. "Hey, Mister Genes, you like teach me today?" They would greet me before school with Hibiscus flowers for my hair and fight to hold my hand as we walked to the class. One sweet young girl, Anola, always brought me a mango from her tree for my lunch. No apples for the teachers in Hawaii. Teaching was more tolerant of affection between teacher and pupil in the 1960s. We didn't have to deal with the "don't touch students" attitude that is so common in today's classroom. I would hold a child on my lap, give hugs, and rub backs when it felt wise to do so. The boys were more difficult to warm to; as even in second grade there is a bit of macho. The Hawaiian culture is largely matriarchal, and the little boys are often spoiled. This was even more evident in the Samoan home.

One special student was Evangelia. He was the scourge of second grade teachers. He was a wiry Samoan boy who saw no reason to attend school. He hated to wear shoes and only did so grudgingly. He talked continually, picked fights, and often left the campus when aggravated. My background at Camp Wediko came in handy when dealing with Evangelia.

My partners and I developed a program that was meant to keep the most truant boys involved in school. With parents and administration permission, I was allowed to take a group of ten of the most difficult boys on a special assignment. Every other day I took my special group out of the classroom for about an hour, usually while others were doing paperwork after lunch. This was a privilege, dependent on attendance and attitude. The first day out, we sat under the shade of a monkey pod tree, took off our shoes, and I suggested that we each have secret names that would be used only in our group. I became Mr. Bear, others were called Gull, Mongoose, Rabbit etc. We called our group the Sea Patrol. I found that I could reinforce most classroom lessons while out on our "patrols." We could take our reading books for lessons in the shade of the trees. Often we would walk to the nearby beach and write our names in the sand or write math problems that had to be solved before a wave washed over them. Other times we would examine the tide pools and try to free the fish that were trapped by the waves. Evangelia amazed me by running barefoot over the coral rocks. He laughed at me and said, "Mr. Bear, I have Samoan feet." He did. His toes gripped the rocks and his leather-like soles flew over the sharp boulders without injury. Tomato Tomato was also in the Sea Patrol and seemed to be coming out of his shell. Should we have called him Snail? The program was a success. Attendance was up, behavior problems were down, and my partner teachers were relieved of discipline problems.

What was not a success was my personal life. Janice said yes to coming to Hawaii, but I'd heard nothing from her for more than two weeks. I was frantic for a letter but frightened about what it may contain.

Few teachers stayed in Nanakuli after classes were dismissed. Most had homes in or near Honolulu. The exception was a group of five student teachers. They had housing near the school and were only a year younger than I. All were of Japanese extraction, intelligent, and to my New England eye, exotic. Among them was a small delicate girl named Lane Fujimori. She was a native of Maui and she, too, was homesick. We became friendly and would share a beer while listening to music. I told her of Janice, New Hampshire, and my increasing "Rock Fever" which one gets after a drive around the island in a half day. I no longer had access to our GSA Nash Rambler, so I purchased a used car with my first paycheck, a Toyota. I'd never heard of Toyota at the time, but they became my auto of choice for years to come. I had little money for fuel and usually I walked to and from school.

One evening there was a mandatory school function. While walking home along the dark beach, I encountered a group of locals. "There a haolie on the beach man," one of them said in pidgin. I knew I should have driven, but it was too late. The group of eight stood in a very threatening semi-circle as if ready to throw me into the sea or bury me in the sand. To my relief, I heard one of them say, "That Mr. Genes, he my sista teacher, he okay man." I shared a Primo and they escorted me down the beach for my protection. That was not my only beach incident.

I enjoyed body surfing when I had some time off. I couldn't afford a real surf board and Nanakuli Beach had a vicious shore break that made board surfing difficult at best. One Saturday afternoon, we had incredibly large storm waves pounding the shore. They must have been ten to twelve feet. I was at the beach with Lorrie and enjoying the surf with some of the older boys from school. I really relished swimming up an incoming wave, flipping backward on the crest, and sliding down the backside. We were having a great time, when the boys suddenly yelled, "Tsunami." I knew what that meant. The wisest practice was to swim beyond the incoming wave before it could form a crest and break. The school boys had fins and were much more skilled in the heavy surf than I. I swam for all I was worth toward the approaching wall of water, but was too slow. A twenty foot breaker released tons of energy right in front of me. I was pulled to the sand and tossed like laundry on the spin cycle. I popped to the surface, only to have the undertow drag me down once again smashing me to the sand. I knew not to panic in these situations and tried to remain focused and calm. Again I rose in the foam only to face another giant. This set of waves came in a series of four. The last wave pulled me under before I had a full breath and would not let go. Okay, time to panic. I fought for the surface and just when I could hold on no more, I found the sky. Looking seaward there were only a few kindly swells. Exhausted, I collapsed on the beach, spitting salt water and sand. Lorrie said, "That was awesome." She never knew of my terror and embarrassment at being so careless in such huge surf.

Life at school remained fulfilling while my down time in my tiny shack was very lonely. I heard nothing from Janice in weeks and was desperate for news. Finally after many sleepless nights, I went over to Lorrie and Lacy's apartment to call Janice. Hawaii to New Hampshire calls were incredibly expensive. To make matters worse, I called person to person. I promised the girls I could pay the bill. I reached the dorm phone and after some confusion, Janice came on the line. She was crying and said, "Didn't you get my letters?"

"No, I didn't," I said.

"Well, I can't come to Hawaii," she mumbled. I asked why, but in truth I could think of a dozen reasons. I had been playing out various scenarios for weeks. It was too expensive, she needed to finish school and, worst of all, and she just didn't care that much about me. I was shaken. I missed home and all that was familiar to me. I was isolated from VISTA now, and felt I had no reason to remain in Hawaii. It was foreign to me. The people were different, the accents were different, even the rocks and vegetation were different.

The next few weeks, I was in a defeatist mood. Life just was not going the way I had hoped. The days went by slowly, the nights were long and lonely. Lorrie and the student teacher, Lane, were my only friends and I poured out my heart to them, but they both had their own worries. I went to the local post office and found a handful of undelivered letters from my parents but, most importantly, from Janice. In them, she explained that her dad and her college Dean convinced her that she should stay in school and finish her education. If we were meant to be, it would happen when I returned.

September and October dragged by as I struggled to pay my bills. Teaching was my refuge. One of my favorite girls was Alana. She was a tall, thin second grader from a strong fundamentalist Christian home. She loved reading to me and always demanded my full attention. Her small home was right next to my one room cottage. At times she would peek in my door and say hello. I was astounded when one morning Alana announced to the entire class, "I saw Mr. Genes and he drinking beer." No privacy in Nanakuli. I kept my door closed more often after this incident. There is a Hawaiian saying about privacy. "You can't shit on one side of the Island without smelling it on the other." I should have heeded the warning.

Our three-on-two program was a limited success. I felt that my second grade experiment was working out well. Others were not convinced. Too many teachers were unwilling to give up control of their kingdoms. Fred C, our principal, was under extreme pressure from the State Department of Education to have this program thrive. A few other staff members and I occasionally accompanied Fred to an out of town bar in a place called Pokia Bay. Because everyone knew and respected Fred, we were served the best pupu (free food served with drinks). Pokia Bay was an R and R site for soldiers on leave from Vietnam (as well as teachers from Nanaikapono). The ongoing war was brought front and center to me. I saw the faraway looks on the drunken boys' faces, knowing they were soon to return to the front lines. I was their age, so I became more and more thankful that I was not eligible to serve, but had a strong sense of guilt as well.

My friend Larry, the Vista volunteer from West Virginia, came to visit and asked if he could camp in my cottage for a few days. I sure could use the company so I said, "of course." Larry had just received his induction notice from his draft board and was to report the following month. VISTA was not recognized by his draft board as a deferment. He was seriously thinking of refusing induction. We spent many hours that week debating the rights and wrongs of our foreign policy. I had been on the fence but after the week with Larry I could not justify our actions in South East Asia. Larry returned to his home, and I never heard from him again.

Our friend, Al Kianoa, invited the girls and me to a beach party at his home in Makaha. It began on Friday night and ended God knows when. There was plenty of beer, food, and Pidgin speak. The guests were mostly Al's surfing and lifeguard friends. I silently slipped into the background and observed the Hawaiians at play, and did they ever play hard. One mainland couple drew my attention. The woman was gorgeous and the man seemed somehow familiar to me. They were having a heated argument, and he seemed about to slap her. He instead, tore off her sunglasses, broke them, and threw them off the porch. I couldn't help but stare. I had never witnessed a man being this aggressive toward a woman. He caught my eye, as if to say, "Stay out of this, or you're next." I left the area and told Lorrie about it. "Don't you know who that is?" she asked. "Who?" I said. "That guy is named Belinsky. He was rookie of the year for the Anaheim

Angles, and she was a Miss Playmate. He could have ripped you apart." I spent the night sleeping on the deck, having had too much to drink to drive back to Nanakuli. The next morning some of the Kanakas went snorkeling and brought back fish to make aku-head stew. "Don't ask what's in it, just eat and enjoy," said big Al. And enjoy I did. When I left that afternoon, I was greeted by a bear of a man speaking pidgin. "So long, Bra" he said as he gave me the hang loose sign. He was the legendary surfer, Buffalo Keaulana, who was often seen on Wide World of Sports and was known as the "Mayor of Makaha." I left feeling accepted in this unfamiliar world.

There were other diversions for me in Nanakuli, but nothing took a bite out of my homesickness. The fall season brought rain squalls rolling in from the Pacific forcing me to put out buckets to catch the rain dripping, and sometimes flowing through my porous home. The cabin seemed to have more than its share of wildlife. Mice, spiders, invading ants, and termites were leaving dust piles on the floor. The cottage wasn't long for this world, and I wasn't long for Hawaii. I had completed my course work at the University of Hawaii, had developed the special "Sea Patrol" class that made school worthwhile for uninvolved boys, and the physical activity-reading program was successful, but I felt defeated. I went to see Fred C. He was not only my first administrator but also the best. He wanted to do what was right for me. He said he could continue my programs with the help of local Hawaiian staff and thanked me for my work. We decided that I would leave during the Thanksgiving break. My kids were very upset, but I assured them that I would miss them much more that they would me. During my last day at Nanaikapono, I was showered with leis of hibiscus and plumeria that the girls picked from the schoolyard. I hugged each of the kids (even Evangelia), my fellow teachers, Lorrie and Lacy, and headed back to New Hampshire with my tail between my legs. Sadder but wiser.

CHAPTER 4

DUBLIN ELEMENTARY

My homecoming thrilled my family, but I was disappointed to be returning home without fulfilling my obligations. I not only quit VISTA, but backed out of my first teaching job. My limited funds were spent on the plane flight from Hawaii to Boston. I sold the Toyota to pay my phone bill and put a down payment on a used car. I had no direction and no prospects. I did, however, have a teaching credential and was not about to be drafted. Things could have been worse.

After Thanksgiving in Derry, I headed to Keene in an eight- year-old beige Ford Falcone, (a real chick magnet). I needed to find a job, an apartment, and Janice. Luckily a fraternity brother was looking to share his very small apartment over a century old garage. It was a tight fit, but offered me my own room and it was inexpensive. My roommate, Dave, was student teaching and seldom home.

Finding Janice was also easy. She was still on campus living in the dorm. We drove around town talking and trying to digest the past six months. In the end, I realized that it was as much homesickness as it was Janice that drove me back to the security of New Hampshire. I was at home with the rolling granite hills, the change of seasons, and the closeness of friends and family. Janice and I agreed to see other people and began the downward slope that leads to ending relationships. She was soon dating a former frat brother, and I enjoyed the freedom that comes from not being tied down.

I returned to the Keene State Job Placement office and was thrilled to discover that there were several teaching possibilities available. A former classmate of mine, Jim Grant, had been offered an administrative position and needed to be replaced ASAP. Better still, the job was just twenty miles from Keene in the small town of Dublin. If I accepted the position, I'd teach fifth and sixth grade math and science, and have my fifth grade homeroom where I would instruct in reading and physical education. The sixth grade teacher would have her homeroom and teach writing, art, and social studies. The superintendent of the Contoocook Valley Consolidated School District, (very wordy for such a small district) called me for a job interview. He seemed pleased with my references, education, and demeanor. His concern was why I had quit my contract in Hawaii. After an honest explanation, he offered me the job subject upon of the approval the school Principal, Mrs. Alice Clucky. Herein lay the rub.

Alice Clucky was everything that Fred Cacholla was not. She was masterfully in charge of her six room school and felt threatened by any changes. She had been there for longer than the dirt in the playground and looked the part. Picture the cliché schoolmarm of the 1950s, Bingo, now you know Mrs. Clucky. She was not pleased with me from the start, because I had a mustache of all things. She let the superintendent know that in no uncertain terms. However reluctantly, she agreed to have me on her staff. On the ride back to Keene the likable administrator told me not to let Mrs. Clucky trouble me, just call him if I had any difficulties.

Dublin is a small town in Southwestern New Hampshire. It is your typical New England village and sits beneath the granite topped Mt. Monadnock. The famous Yankee Magazine is published there, and in the 1910s the town was known as a summer home to the likes of Mark Twain and Henry James. The red brick school building had six classrooms, one for each grade in the building. The children were all freshly scrubbed and lily white, a far cry from my Hawaiian and Samoan students whom I dearly missed. Something was nagging at me and pulling me back toward the west. Was New Hampshire too conservative, too homogenous, and frankly too boring? None the less I was going to do my best with this new assignment.

Unlike casual Hawaii, at Dublin Elementary I dressed in a sport coat and tie. My fifth grade homeroom had a good mix of girls and boys and was a relatively manageable size with twenty-four children. I was replacing a dearly beloved teacher in Mr. Grant, and knew I had to find my own individuality and not try to out teach, out clown, or out shine him. I was wildly successful at that. Mr. Grant gave out over the counter multivitamins to his students (with parent permission), and I continued this practice. What I did not continue was taking them myself without water and sucking until they were dissolved. I tried it for the first week, then decided vomiting in front of fifth graders was not wise—as much as they would have relished it.

I really enjoyed the children and loved teaching math and science. I was a poor math student during my elementary school days and in a strange way this helped me reach the students. I had a background in the "new math" that was being taught at the time. I also tried positive reinforcement as much as possible. I graded papers as I moved about the classroom correcting work as I went. My student's papers didn't have large red Xs all over but instead had big smiling faces or stickers. I seldom called a student out in front of the class for failing an assignment but would have a quite conference at my desk. I enjoyed having an active classroom where students were allowed, indeed, encouraged to talk to each other and move about. I often rearranged desks for student assignments, and had my best students work with those who were having difficulty. In short, I had a noisy and active classroom. Mrs. Clucky was not always pleased with my methods, but then I was not always pleased with Mrs. Clucky either.

The small village of Dublin sits on a hill and is subject to cold winds and freezing temperatures. Mrs. Clucky had a rule that recess was to be held outside unless the temperature was below ten degrees Fahrenheit. There was no taking into account wind chill. I often had to stand with my back to the wind with ten or more children huddled around me for warmth. We looked like the emperor penguins in "Walk of the Penguins." *Brrr*!

I learned how careful a teacher must be when dealing with pre-adolescent girls. One morning I bent down to pick up a dropped a pencil and my eyes locked onto the red face of one of my better female students. She assumed I dropped the pencil on purpose in order to look up her skirt. She gossiped about this incident to others in her clique, and it got back to me via my teaching partner. The last thing I needed was for this to get to some of the parents. I went to Mrs. Clucky and told her about this. She was actually understanding. She said that girls this age are so insecure about their bodies that projecting blame on others is common. I became much more aware of the psychology of preteen girls.

Science was a joy to teach. I had access to audio visual equipment, a small science lab, and the great outdoors. We would go for nature walks in the deep NH woods, collecting insects, seeds, grasses, etc... I was also happy to provide a science fair for my students. They had individual projects which were displayed during the parental open house, complete with ribbons and small trophies for the top displays. One day, while beginning an experiment from the chemical lab, I was demonstrating how to insert a glass tube into a rubber stopper. I did so very poorly. Instead of having the glass tube in the stopper, it broke and was neatly inserted into the palm of my hand. I merely said "this is not the way it is done" as I freely bled on the floor. A lesson in first aid seemed more appropriate at that moment.

In the spring as the temperatures began to warm and the maple sap was running, I began a lesson on space exploration and jet propulsion. Americans had not yet gone to the moon, but the race was on. I wanted to demonstrate how the Saturn Rocket would propel a manned capsule into space. My capsule was to be an oil can into which we packed a mixture that would burn when heated. The experiment came from a science education periodical. What could go wrong? We attached the oilcan filled with the magic powder to a wire that ran across the playground. I had the children all stand behind me as I lit a small blowtorch and held it up to the can. Now, in theory, the powder would ignite and the gas would escape from the spout thus propelling the "spaceship" down the wire. In reality I had just made a small bomb and it acted just like one. There was a horrific explosion and our capsule broke into two pieces, one of which flew over the school building and landed on Highway 102. I herded the very excited class into the building. Most of them thought that was a really cool demonstration. I just hoped that no one had seen me trying to blow up the town. It was never mentioned to me and the kids, bless them, remained quiet about it. I still shudder to think of what may have happened to one of the children not to mention my career. From that time on, I was much more careful with the welfare and safety of my students.

During the spring of 1969, I began to let my imagination wander. Did I really want to stay in New Hampshire and continue teaching? Was there another path? I wrote to several colleges for information on a master's degree program. I'm not sure why, but the field of Vocational Rehabilitation seemed to draw me in. I enjoyed the psychology classes I'd taken and felt that counseling would be a good fit for me. I would still be dealing with disabilities and would not be in a classroom year after year. Two schools stood out for me. One was Florida State University in Tallahassee and the other was the University of Northern Colorado in Greeley. I had little funds but there was a traineeship available. If I were to get it, I would be provided with tuition and a small stipend for housing, books, and food. I wrote to Greeley inquiring about this possibility. To my surprise they wrote back saying I was accepted into the program, and I *may* be eligible for the grant. I was very excited at the possibility of heading back west and of getting an advanced degree. There was really nothing holding me back from exploring new vistas. I had a causal relationship with a girl at Keene State, but it was going nowhere. Teaching in Dublin was a great experience, but the money was poor and I was getting wanderlust again. Now, how could I afford the move? I did some research and found that the Elks Club had a scholarship available to those in graduate school programs dealing with Cerebral Palsy. Certainly Vocational Rehab fit the bill. My Uncle Harvey in Keene was an Elk and the local chapter agreed to sponsor me. I applied through them and was surprised to be rewarded a six hundred dollar prize, which in 1969 was a sizable gift. I saved all I could from my teaching salary and inquired about working the summer at Camp Wediko again.

On the last day of school we scheduled a picnic and outdoor games for all the classes. I volunteered my students to help with games for the younger students. We made small certificates for them and had activities they all could participate in. The fun was to begin after the ten o'clock recess. My fifth graders had done really well during the last month of school and we left the classroom fifteen minutes early to set up the games for the younger children. Mrs. Clucky would have none of it. She called me into her room as my teaching partner took over my class. In short, she said I had been disrespectful to her authority from the beginning and that she hoped I had a different attitude next year. I took this wonderful opportunity to tell her, "I'm not going to be here next year and thanks for the advice." I had burned another bridge and was headed to Colorado. I did explain to my supervisor what happened, and he said not to worry, he would always give me a very positive recommendation.

I was able to return to Camp Wediko for the summer. Most of the counselors were new as were the campers, however the clinical staff were much the same. A friend of mine from high school also spent the summer at the camp with my recommendation. I was partnered with a wonderful lively Irishman named Milo. He was long-haired, short tempered, and an incredibly colorful personality. When we led our campers into the mess hall Milo would lead us in singing, "The Rocky Road to Dublin." This year, in addition to serving as the camping instructor, I was assigned a cabin of twelve boys that Milo and I supervised. Two of our boys were from Harlem and had never been out of the city. Getting them to quiet down at night was a chore left up to me. With lights out I would begin telling them my version of the "Hobbit" and later the "Lord of the Rings." It was a condensed version, but it sure was an effective lights out ploy. I always left them hanging with "We will continue the story tomorrow night and see if Smaug wakes up." I managed to use this type of line for the entire summer.

The last week of the summer I planned to take a select group of boys on a real camping trip. This had never been done at camp, and I really had to sell the project to the clinical staff as well as most of the counselors. Milo would join eight campers and me as we headed into the White Mountain National Forest in two camp station wagons. All went well at first. We hiked in Franconia Notch, saw the Old Man of the Mountain (now defunct), and ate hot dogs cooked over the open fire. Lights out meant another story. This time it was "Three Fingered Willy," then we all settled down for the night. Drip, drip, drip, at midnight the rain began. Drip, splash, and then water was pooling in the canvas tent. I packed up my clothing and along with my tent-mate headed for the car. Crack, thunder shook our site and then the rain became a downpour. Soon two campers in a car became six. Then the other car filled with Milo and the rest of our sodden group. Bad news: we all got soaked. Good news: the boys were able to joke about it and returned to camp the next day as heroes.

That year camp was full of animal adventures. There was an amazing camp goat named Jonathan who would barge through our screen door each morning and accompany my campers to breakfast. His timing was uncanny and the kids loved him. We also had a camp cat who we named after one of the camp nurses Susan Ann Stevens. So "Sass" was the given name of the feline. The tongue in cheek joke was that everyone knows the cat Sass. One morning just before breakfast a camper ran toward the mess hall with one of our "have-a-heart traps." "Guess what I caught," he screamed. It seemed all fifty or so campers ran toward him as all the staff ran in the other direction. He had trapped a small skunk. Luckily it was not threatened and was released with its perfume intact.

It was during that summer that the staff gathered in the old staff home and watched Neil Armstrong take the "small step for a man." As camp wound down I became more and more excited about graduate school. I was going to Greeley and even if I didn't receive the traineeship, I would somehow manage this move. I believe this is when my mother said, "Gene ran away from home." I relished being the black sheep of the family.

CHAPTER 5

GREELEY, COLORADO

I packed up my lovely beige ford Falcon which had all the sex appeal of Yasser Arafat, and along with my high school friend, Ben, headed west. This is not a travel log so I won't get into the details of our journey other than to say that Toad Suck Ferry, Arkansas was not friendly to long-haired bearded Yankees. We went through the Blue Ridge Parkway, the Tennessee Valley, the Texas panhandle, Los Alamos NM, and on to Vegas. Just two wild and crazy guys on the great American road. All went well until we made our way to Tijuana. Without going into details, too much tequila and a Tijuana taxi can lead to *mucho* trouble. Luckily we did not carry much cash because we were relieved of all we had in our possession. We spent the following night in Disneyland feeling much more safe and secure. Minnie Mouse looked pretty hot that night. We rolled up to the Bay Area and stayed with Ben's brother north of San Francisco. It was then across Nevada and on to Colorado.

All the brochures I had from Greeley looked as if the city was the gateway to the Rockies. I was disheartened to see a sign stating "Greeley 10 miles." It was flat as a pancake here and what was that awful smell? When the sun rose the next morning I saw Greeley for the first time. It looked more like Kansas than my preconception of Colorado. The smell was twofold; first there is a sugar beet processing plant on the outskirts of town and second, Greeley had the world's largest feedlot right within the city limits. As a friend once said, "When you have a hundred thousand head of cattle together one of them is bound to smell bad." He also described the Greeley weather forecast by stating in his best weatherman voice, "Today it is going to cloud up and shit." The Colorado Rockies were at least fifty miles to the west and indeed eastern Colorado looks much like western Kansas. Another hidden fact: Greeley was founded by a temperance society and named after Horace Greeley who once said, "Go west young man." Bottom line, Greeley was a dry town. No alcohol was to be sold in town. This was my home for the next year. I soon found that although alcohol can't be bought in town, nothing stopped one from drinking in town.

I went to the student union on campus and found a housing board with short term rentals available for the week before school opened. I joined three other students staying in a basement apartment, but would stay in the upperclassman dorm when school began. I walked around the campus and was impressed with the facilities. Keene State had fifteen hundred students while Northern Colorado had fifteen *thousand*. I walked casually downtown to get acquainted with the city. While walking down the main street someone I had never seen before said, "Good morning." I looked at him dumbly and thought "Who are you?" This was one of my first lessons on the difference between New England and the Mountain West. New Hampshire reserve in 1969 did not allow saying "Hello" to total strangers. We just didn't do that. I had a lot to learn.

I was accepted into the Vocational Rehab program but still did not have the necessary funds. I made an appointment with a Dr. Turner who was my advisor. He thought that I had a good chance of being awarded the traineeship because they were trying to attract more students from back east, but he gave no promises. Three days later I received notice that indeed I was awarded the money; tuition and dorm fees were paid for. I needed funds for meals, books, and the other living necessities. I soon discovered that most of the students in the Vocational Rehab program were rewarded the traineeships— I was nothing special.

I moved into Turner Hall the day before classes began and met my new roommates, Jim Frustaci, an education major, Dick Lempke, a music major, and Bill Whipple, a major pain in the ass. I was the only graduate student in the group. I was immediately aware of my New Hampshire accent. It became a sticking point during my entire stay in Colorado. "Let's go get a beea, or I'll drive my caa." We New Englanders seem to misplace our "Rs." For all of those I leave out I graciously add one to words like Linder (Linda) or maybe a Pander (Panda). I soon learned to say "sack" instead of "bag," and "Pop" instead of "tonic." I was happily surprised with the dorm. The floors alternated between Men's and Women's levels. Students had no restrictions or curfews. Alcohol consumption was not regulated either. In spite of Greeley being a dry town, the neighboring towns were anything but. I'm sure there were some drugs around the school, but I never saw any.

My first classroom experience was eye opening. At twenty-two, I was the youngest and the least experienced student in the program. My palms were sweating profusely as I tried to hold my panic inside. I knew no one in the entire state, not just in the classroom. We introduced ourselves, stating our background and why we wished to have Vocational Rehabilitation as a career. I spouted out what I thought they wanted to hear. The program would take at least four quarters of study followed by comprehensive exams and then a full quarter in a supervised traineeship. Most of the classes would be graduate level and directly related to vocational counseling, however, we would also be taking some upper level undergraduate courses, such as statistics, foundations of counseling, and the nature of disabilities. My fellow students included a totally blind man, one with post-polio paralysis, and others who had served in the Military or had been employed in probation-parole. We even had a former priest. Most were from the Mountain West and none lived in the college dorms. The good news was that we were all beginning the program together and hopefully would have study groups together. I sure hoped that I could fit in with this eclectic group. The Vocational Rehab staff consisted of a handful of professors including my advisor. The majority of our classes would be taught by the Vocational Rehab staff. The first thing the professors did for us was organize a party along with a keg. Even the Mormon, Dr. Eldridge chipped in, but let it be known that his money only provided the pretzels.

The first quarter flew by all too quickly. I was able to hold my own in the classroom and enjoyed hanging out with fellow students. One of my classmates was Gary Aanes who had been a parole officer. He became a mentor for me. Through Gary I met some great friends. I fondly remember my first Mexican meal. A fellow student named Dan Torres took us to a restaurant in a small Hispanic town near Greeley. He ordered menudo for all. With my limited culinary background, I thought that Mexican food consisted of chili and taco chips. I managed to down the menudo as my face turned red and sweat ran down my shirt like rain on a windshield. I don't think I've had menudo since, but I do thank Dan for my introduction to spice, *and* margaritas to sooth the fire.

Another notable character in our program was Mat Sherwood. He truly scared me. He came from the high desert lands of Western Colorado, and he looked like a modern Teddy Roosevelt. He was loud, belligerent, and wildly popular. Gary warned me to stay away from Mat if he was drinking. He often was, and I did.

We had other characters and they made me feel welcome. Ed was a tall soft spoken former athlete, Grace had worked as a bartender in Wyoming, Danny was a cowboy from Montana who left the program when he was accepted as a farrier, Bucky was a married student who had worked as a cop, Tom was married to a beautiful nurse and he played guitar in local clubs, and Ryan who had been a DJ in Nebraska and would keep us in stitches with his antics. I'm sure I was somewhat of an oddity to them.

Some of the required classes were also part of the Special Education curriculum, and I was very comfortable with these. One of these was "Psychology of the Disabled," and was taught by a revered professor. She was totally blind and had an incredible gift of organization. Each student was assigned a seat and she memorized the placement. When she called on you, she uncannily stared straight at you and you had better be seated in the proper place. During the second quarter I took a Rehab class with Dr. Eldridge. He chose four students to give their philosophy of life. Luckily, I was not one of the chosen few. Dr. Eldridge led off by giving us an hour lecture directly from the book of Mormon. He then let us know that now we had heard, "the word," and could either accept it or burn forever in hell. One of my classmates strenuously objected to the manner in which the class was being run and told Dr. Eldridge just that. He received a "C" grade for the class which in graduate school is failure. Another of the chosen students was Ray. He was in his mid-thirties, and was very intelligent, but aloof. A man of a mystery. He seemed very nervous as he began his presentation with, "I hope you won't think less of me, but I am a Catholic priest." We were flabbergasted. It seems Ray was a Jesuit priest from Texas and he ran into difficulties with the Bishop. He disobeyed orders and was excommunicated. "I still consider myself a man of God" he stated. Ray became a friend to all of us after his presentation. He was so much more honorable than Dr. Eldridge had been.

I had another run-in with our LDS professor. He lectured in a required statistics class. I was certain that I had earned an "A". When I saw my grades, I received an "A" in every class *except* statistics. When I spoke to Dr. Eldridge about this he smiled and said, "If I gave you an "A" you'd have gotten a 4.0 and you are not a 4.0 student." He then added, "If it makes you feel any better, you got the highest "B" in the class." Thanks a bunch!

Time away from the classroom was spent studying, but I also enjoyed some of the experiences that Colorado offered. I joined the Ski Club and because I was a graduate student, I was able to act as a chaperone. That was a farce, but I got to go on trips for half price. We skied Loveland, Arapahoe, Breckenridge, Vail, and Steamboat. I learned to maneuver through fluffy powder, dodge trees in the glades, and to fall gracefully. Gary Aanes and I began running at the University Track in order to trim some of our extra poundage. We struggled to a four lap mile then would retreat to the Student Union for a burger. After attending Keene State it was fun to be on a large campus and witness the various NCAA sporting events. The University of Northern Colorado was not known for its sports teams with one exception. They were highly competitive in wrestling. I never witnessed major college wrestling and was quiet taken with it. My roommate, John, would invite me to wrestle against him in the dorm. He was maybe 125 pounds, but he put the hammer down each time, leaving me flat on my back.

Our small dorm apartment with four students was not conducive for studying. Two music majors can be loud mates. We also had a Bebe Parrot living with us. Okay, he was my pet and I named him Clancy. He did provide hours of entertainment. I longed to get into the Rockies for hiking, but the snow comes quickly to Colorado in the fall and I had a long wait before throwing on a backpack and heading to the high elevations. From our dorm room I looked upward to Long's Peak and made it my goal to reach its fourteen thousand foot summit.

The holidays came, and I was invited to spend Thanksgiving with my roommate, John, at his Denver home. His family is Italian and I fell in love with his grandmother. She took an empty wine glass as an insult, and I tried to be well mannered. Christmas break was for two weeks and my car was not up to the drive home, indeed it barely made it around Greeley. There was a ride sharing board at the student union and I found a student from Vermont who wanted passengers. Three of us shared the driving and the expenses. We drove straight through, stopping only for gas and snacks. One person driving, one as wing man to keep the driver awake, and one asleep in the back seat. Thirty-three hours later, I met my father in Manchester. Two weeks of eating and visiting family and friends, and I was back in the car for another thirty-three hours of boring highway travel. Never again!

During the next quarter, our class went on a field trip to Craig Rehabilitation Hospital in Denver. Craig is regarded as one of the best spinal-cord and traumatic brain injury rehabilitation facilities in the country. Rehab counselors in Colorado often worked with the patients from this fine hospital. We saw firsthand how challenging a brain or spinal cord injury could be. It would be a Vocational Rehabilitation counselor's job to find suitable employment for these patients. This was my first experience with brain and spinal cord injuries, and I was impressed at the patients' endurance and spirit. One young mother in her early thirties who had suffered a massive stoke was on a standing table. She had such a wonderful smile beneath the pain, and I was particularly impressed by her.

During the spring quarter, I took an undergraduate elective class in criminology. Many rehab counselors have to work with former incarcerated clients, and I thought this class would be both interesting and important. We were asked to present a paper detailing an interview with a correction officer. Gary Aanes, who had been a probation officer, arranged a meeting with a former coworker. I called his friend Jason, and he invited me to accompany him for some pre-parole interviews at Canon City Penitentiary. I jumped at the chance. During the drive I discovered what his job entailed and what the plan for the day would be. At the gate a guard looked at me and asked Jason, "Bringing me new meat?" That alone scared me as the large iron gates slammed behind us. Jason had four interviews to conduct and I sat with him taking notes. The first three were uneventful. The inmates all were eligible for parole and gave answers they were sure Jason wanted to hear. Our fourth interview took place in the maximum confinement unit. Once again I was uneasy passing through iron gates and being eyed by inmates with suspicion, or was it lust? In the small interview room a handcuffed inmate was seated at a table as we entered. A guard stood to the side and watched intently. The inmate was wild eyed and jumpy. He did answer the usual questions with the usual canned answers. Yes, he was sorry for his crimes, he did his time, he had family to go to, and he wanted to find a good job. When Jason asked if he had anything to add. He smiled and said, "I'm still going to get him." Jason asked, "Who are you going to get?" His reply, "Roy Rodgers and his bitch Dale Evans, he is my real Daddy and he never comes to see me." This was a brief look into this convict's delusions. Jason told me, "I think we can be sure he is going to stay put for the foreseeable future." I bet Roy and Dale were relieved.

We had a substitute professor who taught a required course in Rehab law and vocational casework. He was a "by the book" guy and very boring. Our entire grade would be based on his final exam. We had a study group that met two or three times a week. Bucky, a partner in the study group, had a friend who was a recent graduate of our program. He shared a corrected test from the same course. We used it in our study group, of course. When the final exam was passed out, we gave out a collective gasp. It was the exact same test we had studied, word for word. It was not an easy exam, in fact, it was damn difficult, but we knew the answers. The final results were remarkable. Half the class aced it (our study group), the other half barely passed. Bottom line: those that did really well were accused of cheating, and we were called before the department chairman. We explained that we had a study test from a previous class and, if anything, should be admired for doing good research. He actually agreed with us and chastised the instructor for not preparing his own exam.

In the third quarter all the concerns in department were about the comprehensive exams which would be given in late May. These were taken in one day, a standard multiple choice exam in the morning and an essay portion in the afternoon. Because it was given during finals week, I had four or five days off to study. I headed to the mountains with my books and notes. Rocky Mountain National Park is fifty miles from Greeley, and I headed for the solitude of Bear Lake. I was lured by the trail, put the books aside, and headed up past eleven thousand feet where I opened my first beer. My second beer was costly. The unfamiliar altitude and the alcohol didn't mix well. My stomach involuntarily emptied. I went to a more comfortable level to study. The comp exams were difficult but our professors had prepared us well. When the stressful exams were done most in our program went out to celebrate at a Mexican restaurant. It was a Margareta night. One not to forget, if only I could remember.

The pressure was off for the summer quarter classes. I moved out of the dorm and shared a small apartment with Gary Aanes. The parrot went to my former roommate, Rick. The classes were more of the same with the exception of a counseling class where we had actual counseling experience using our best Rogarian techniques. "I feel tense." "So you feel tense?" Pause.

"My classes suck.' "You feel your classes suck?" You get the idea.

Gary and I got along well. He was more experienced than I, having worked in probation—parole. He did have a difficult period when he found that a prisoner had been released. Gary helped deny this inmate's parole and had been threatened by him. All ended well when the inmate was incarcerated once again in a matter of weeks, and Gary could now relax.

The most vital task that summer was finding a placement for my internship. The internship is a requirement for graduation. It would last from the first of September until the Christmas break and the conclusion of our Master's Program. We would work under supervision as counselors in a Rehab setting of our choice. I wanted to stay in Colorado and eventually work there in Vocational Rehab. However, my advisor said that the state had few opportunities because of a limited budget. He suggested that I try elsewhere. Most of my peers were Colorado residents and did not want to displace their families. I understood, but if not Colorado, where? I was not going to return to New Hampshire again with a feeling of retreat. I contacted several programs in Northern California and received a response with an intriguing proposition from Napa State Hospital.

Napa State is a large psychiatric hospital located in the wine producing region of the famous Napa Valley. I was very interested, and talked to my supervisor about the possibility. He made a call to the program director in Napa and they said they would be happy to have me. I had only the summer session to be in Colorado, and I hoped to make the best of it.

The campus was much quieter in the summer. Most undergraduates had returned home and the professors had a casual attitude. I had only a few required courses and used my electives for courses that were of interest to me, such as abnormal psychology. I managed to take some time off to head to the high country whenever I could. Gary's girlfriend, Audrey, was a constant companion that summer. There was never a dull moment when she was around. I fondly remember a dinner prepared for us by two friends of Audrey's from Ethiopia. I can still taste the dura wat.

Two good friends from NH joined me to tackle the trail to Long's Peak. My friends showed up on a Friday and the following morning bright and early we head for Rocky Mountain National Park to begin our climb. I felt great during the hike because I had been living a mile above sea level for over a year. My friends, who lived near sea level, did not fare as well. We did make the top, but two of three were green and emptied their stomach shortly before the fourteen thousand foot summit. I bid them goodbye the following day and prepared for my own upcoming trip to California. I was in contact with the Napa State Hospital Rehab staff, and I had finalized plans for my three month internship.

The week before I was to leave Colorado, I had tickets for a Rod McKuen concert at the Red Rocks Amphitheater above Denver. At the time, he was one of the nation's leading poets, songwriters, and singers. His sappy lyrics and poems always touched me. "Stanyan Street and Other Sorrows" how could you not be moved, even if told in his raspy sentimental voice. I was now headed to the Bay Area where Rod lived. As I strode up the hill to the entrance, a teenage girl was standing on a nearby red rock outcropping and screaming hysterically. A hundred or more concert goers just passed her by. No one seemed inclined to help. I asked her what the trouble was. "It's a big rattlesnake," she mumbled. I carefully walked over to her, grabbed her shaking hand, and walked her back to the safety of asphalt. She thanked me and disappeared. I never did see the snake but was astounded that so many people walked by without caring.

Red Rocks Amphitheater sits high above Denver in the foothills and is a magical venue for music. I was surprised to see a friend and classmate, Mike, from North Dakota. He was there with his fiancée and her sister, Vivian. I knew Vivian from the dormitory and always found her both attractive and lots of fun. I joined the three of them for the show. After the opening act and as the sun set, Rod came on and began his poetry reading and songs. He seemed so genuine and warm that even the most cynical critics had to have been moved. His encore number was maybe his biggest or only hit, "Jean." Now Vivian must have thought the song was "Gene." She snuggled really close to me and held my hand as tears rolled down her cheeks. Was I missing something? Mike's brother was a security guard at the show and he said, "Let's go back stage and meet Rod." Why not? We moved to the backstage and sure enough there was Rod McKuen. He was talking to a young, blind, multiply-disabled girl. This confirmed my admiration of him because he was so gracious and willing to take his time with this girl. We did get to meet him and gave the usual, "Great Show, thanks." Not to my surprise, Vivian asked if I could drive her home. "You bet," was all I could come out with. What a smooth talker I was back then. We sat in the car in front of her parents' home and talked for hours. She was surprised and disappointed that I was taking my internship in California. I left her that night and never saw her again. I still sometimes think, "What if?"

The next week I finished a few term papers, took some final exams, packed my Ford Falcon, and headed west once again.

CHAPTER 6

NAPA STATE HOSPITAL

I had three extra travel days before I was due to report to my assignment in Napa. I headed west via the northern route, through Cheyenne, Casper, the Wind River Mountains and on to the Grand Tetons and Yellowstone. The west just amazes with its grandeur and vastness. I kept hoping that the beige Falcon would hold together as the temperature indicator continued jumping from green to red. My mechanical expertise stops at a screwdriver, so I just kept throwing water in the radiator, downhill good, uphill bad. Mountainous Idaho was challenging, then I rambled across the Palouse of Oregon and down the Pacific Coast on the famous Highway One. Once I got past Eureka, CA, I headed into the majestic Redwoods toward the wine country and on to Napa.

When I was in contact with the Director of Rehab at Napa, I had asked about housing on the hospital grounds. He said he would arrange a room for me at a very modest cost. I gladly accepted because funds were becoming very slim, and Napa is very expensive. The Elks club scholarship ran out and the traineeship money paid my tuition and books with very little left over. I envisioned a room where other interns, or maybe a cadre of student nurses, would be housed. Boy, was I wrong. I was given a small room over the geriatric ward. There were two other rooms on the floor. One was occupied by an older patient who was diagnosed as paranoid schizophrenic. He apparently was not well enough to return to society but could manage in a structured environment. I saw him only fleetingly in my three months at Napa. He gave me a head nod, a quiet "lo," and a door slam. The other room was taken by a former heroin addict who now helped with the Drug Treatment Ward. He was a tattooed behemoth with a shaved head, and he scared the holy be-Jesus out of me. It seemed his heroin dependency was replaced by alcohol. He once invited me to his room for a neighborly drink. He poured straight whiskey into a glass that had last been washed during the Truman Administration. I dared not refuse, and I successfully avoided him from then on. He seemed to have an unending supply of women (mostly patients) visiting his room, and I avoided them as well. I kept telling myself that this situation was temporary, but I had no clue what the future had in store.

"B Ward" was my workplace assignment. It had regular hospital medical and custodial staff, but the counseling staff were from the State Department of Vocational Rehabilitation. The clients (no longer referred to as patients) were from the general hospital population. They were young to middle-aged adults, both male and female, and were housed in separate wings, South Wing for men, North for women. Most were on medication but were being weaned from the strongest drugs whenever possible. These clients were pre-screened on other wards and were believed to be employable once they were released from the hospital. We did pre-vocational counseling as well as teaching social skills necessary for success in the world of work. The ward was run on a behavior modification model, rewarding behavior that met the staff goals. Aberrant behavior had negative consequences, ranging from cigarette restrictions to being returned to the general population. While there was no set time for a stay on the ward, clients were expected to make progress on a weekly basis. They were given work assignments and expected to attend all group and individual counseling sessions. The clients came from the greater Bay Area and would return to their homes where local counselors would continue their cases. Therefore, careful documentation of each client was essential.

The Rehab director was John Manning. He was the supervisor of both the clients and the staff. We had four Rehab counselors on the ward, and I was assigned Ed Merrick as my immediate Supervisor. Ed was a Jerry Garcia look-alike with full red beard, round figure, and a soft voice. He was admired by clients and staff alike. He was even-tempered, never raising his voice, and had a knack of bringing out the best in those around him. I was very fortunate to have him first as a mentor and later as a friend.

My first week on the ward was spent observing Ed and following him from morning till late afternoon. I was introduced to clients and staff alike and was given keys to the ward. I was to guard them with my life. Napa is a huge facility and often patients are allowed to leave their wards and have free access to the grounds. Your keys were your identification, no keys and you were just another patient. The majority of patients were voluntarily committed and could be released at their discretion. It was their choice. Others were court ordered, such as those serving drug sentences. On our ward we had both. Our clients participated in group, as well as individual, counseling. Ed had me read the files of patients on his (and therefore my) caseload. Rehab Counselors are given a yearly budget and it has to be spent wisely according to their clients' needs. These could range from a proper set of work clothes to college courses. Among the notable clients on Ed's caseload were: Carol, a young mother who became so depressed she would not leave her room; Rich, who attacked and raped a nun because "God told him to"; Becky, who self-mutilated slicing herself repeatedly with razor blades; Robbie, a homeless young black man who took so much acid he lost touch with reality; and Sinbad, a huge Black man who heard disturbing voices while in prison. There were others, of course, but these five were representative of our general population.

Mornings began with a report from the night charge nurse. She dictated the report on a small tape recorder. The night nurse Hilda, was the cliché "Big Nurse" from the Cuckoo's Nest. She bossed the clients, the night attendants, and anyone else within shouting distance. At night the ward belonged to her and our *clients* became her *patients*. One morning her night report was given in a near panic-stricken voice. It seems a patient was wandering the ward at two a.m. when "Big Nurse" asked, "And what sir can I do for you at this hour?" Meaning get back to your bed. Instead of taking the obvious hint, our client looked her in the eye and said, "Well I could use a piece of ass." She called security and had him brought to a holding ward. Our staff was rolling on the floor in fits of laughter just wishing we could have been there to see Hilda's reaction first hand. We released our "night stroller" from lock-up, and he was given an additional work assignment. His room was locked at night from then on.

During one of our group counseling sessions things were not going well. Nobody was volunteering any useful insights, both the clients and staff were listless. The sessions were supposed to be vocational in nature. Ed knew that most clients could perform the labor, but the inability to relate to bosses and fellow employees was the difference between keeping and losing jobs. Ed got up from the circular arrangement of chairs and returned with a volleyball. "Let's go have a game." So we did. Ed later told me that some days you just have to mix it up. "You can check a lot of boxes during a volleyball game such as team work, cooperating with others, willingness to share, the ability to fail gracefully, and the ability to win graciously." Ed was a wise man.

I spent a lot of time questioning myself during my time on B Ward. I did well at Greeley overcoming some demons, but was this kind of Rehab work over my head? Clients who had psychotic and/or criminal backgrounds were among the most difficult to place in meaningful employment. I could handle a former soldier amputee or a blinded factory worker. They often had good work incentive, but B Ward clients were much more challenging. In retrospect I learned so much about myself while I was there. I thought that Hawaii was tough, but lonely nights above the geriatric ward were intolerable at times. I had only a small radio and books for company, no cell phones, or laptops back in 1969. I could eat at the ward but usually went into town for food. My first weekend I visited the local wineries that Napa is so famous for and was lucky to have a tour by Louis Martini at the winery that bears his name. He was a delightful eighty-year-old Italian who relished telling stories to anyone with the time to listen. God knows I had the time.

Luckily I had a contact south of San Francisco in the foggy town of Daly City. My brother-in-law's younger brother, Gary, was trying to make a life for himself in the west. He and his wife, Kathy, invited me to spend the weekend with them if I didn't mind sleeping on the floor. I knew Gary only from my sister's wedding when he was best man. I thought of him as a worldly sophistic who once taught dancing for the Arthur Murray studios. I was wrong, Gary was a down to earth, fun loving, and a gracious host. We would often get together on weekends, watch the 49ers, play pick up football, or hike in the Marin hills. I slept on the floor because Gary and Kathy had a friend living with them. Greg was a mountain of a man, at six-foot-five inches and weighing at least three hundred pounds. Greg was a gentle giant. When we first shook hands mine was lost in his huge mitt. Greg was also the first black man who I knew well and could consider a friend. I was lucky to see the see the Bay Area's hidden gems through Gary and Greg's knowledgeable eyes.

The weeks on the ward went by at a snail's pace. The weekends by contrast zipped. One morning I came upon a client sitting in the empty day room. He was chuckling and talking to the wall, not to me. I listened to the ongoing conversation for several moments before he realized I was in the room. He ogled me for a second, smiled, and said, "Hey, I'm having a group meeting." I left him to his voices and admired his sense of humor. Delusions and hallucinations were fairly commonplace on the ward. Often the inner voices were more of a comfort to the clients than those of the staff. Fantasy trumps reality for many of us. I found, however, that most of our clients were friendly, open, and when not under duress, rational.

One morning at our group meeting Carol was visibly upset and softly sobbing. She was willing to share her distress. She was close to her release and was uncertain about facing her small children and her estranged husband. Rich (our nun rapist), who was always inappropriate said, "Carol, why don't you just leave your damn kids." Carol screamed like a banshee, broke her glasses, threw them at Rich, and scrambled to her room. Sinbad, all six-feet-four of mean muscle, threw his chair aside and charged Rich shouting, "I'm going to kill you, mother f*cker." Luckily, and wisely, Rich backed down, way down, in fact he ran. Sinbad, at our insistence, backed off as well and went to comfort Carol. It seems Carol and Sinbad had an ill-advised affair going on. Rich was ordered to his room and was put on restrictions. Sinbad and Carol returned to group and we were successful in calming them, and getting them to discuss the incident and their inappropriate behaviors.

I became friendly with several of our clients, many of whom had beaten their demons, but I tried to keep my professional distance. We would share stories of home and family. I was curious about ward life after the counseling staff left for home. I would sometimes venture to the ward and talk to clients and night staff, have dinner with them, and watch

TV in the common rooms. One of the clients mentioned a weekly dance held in the hospital's recreation hall and said, "You should come and watch." It seemed preferable to staying in my room, so I put down my book and headed for the recreation hall. The dance was not a B Ward activity but was open to hospital patients who had "full campus" privileges. I entered the hall, and watched the few dancers and the many wallflowers. Most of the behaviors were appropriate and, if not, the nursing staff would have patients removed and escorted back to their wards by security if necessary. After a half hour of watching, talking to some of our clients, and drinking watery punch, I headed for the door, preferring my bad book to the bad music. As I reached for the exit a middle-aged nurse with her hair in a tight bun and her face full of authority said, "And where, sir, do you think you are going?"

"Back to my room." I answered.

"Oh, no you're not," she shot back with conviction.

I pulled out my prized keys to show that I was staff. Her eyes grew beady, "And just where, did you get these" she said as she grabbed the keys from my hand. I was flustered, but didn't dare raise my voice as she was about to call security. I calmly explained to this supervising nurse that I was doing my traineeship on B Ward and was staying on campus for financial reasons. After a call to the administration building, I was liberated. Thank God! She let me go with a sneer as if she still wanted to see me in lockup. There is a thin veneer between the sane and the not so sane. We aren't so different. There but for fortune.

One weekend, Ed invited me to his home in the upscale town of Fairfax, just north of San Francisco. His wife, Erika, was born in Germany and had one foot back in the old world. That Friday night the three of us attended an Oktoberfest in Pleasanton. Erika and Ed insisted that I dress in lederhosen, ruffled shirt, and Bavarian hat. Who was I to argue with my supervisor? Erika was friends with the band leader from Germany so we had access to a special barrel of Bavarian Beer. I found my polka feet after two or three liters of the foamy brew.

Ed's passion was sailing, and he insisted that I join him on the bay one Saturday in spite of gale warnings. Sail we did. His open cockpit sailing boat was fast, the swells were high, and I was scared shitless. My job was to stay out of Ed's way, lean toward the high side, hold the beer, and avoid the swinging boom. We had lunch in San Francisco, and I tried to keep it down as we headed homeward downwind to Tiburon. That evening we relaxed with a single malt and a social joint. Ed became more than a supervisor that weekend.

Back on B ward, I was faced with my first one on one unsupervised counseling session. Ed chose Sinbad as my first. Thanks! To say that Sinbad, also known as Carl Weston, was intimidating was a gross understatement. He had NBA tattoos, the build of a pro wrestler, and the perception of a third grader, even though he was a forty-two year old black man. He was doing hard time in a federal penitentiary when he began hearing voices and was therefore sent to a prison dealing with convicts who were unable to function in the general population. After several years of good behavior, he was sent to Napa to finish his time. B ward was his last stop before he gained his freedom. Our role was to prepare him for meaningful employment. He had to be able to listen to others in a non-threatening manner, follow directions, and live within a society that he had once rejected. He would be on probation and would have to deal with his probation officer as well as a rehab counselor. Voc. Rehab was sending him to classes at a local junior college in general studies. He walked to the campus but returned to the ward when classes were done. I found him to be intelligent but extremely naïve.

We knew each other from group counseling sessions, but had seldom spoken one-on-one. We met in one of the counseling rooms, which was small with only a desk and two chairs. That morning, I had imbibed in one too many coffees and I felt a strange buzz in my over caffeinated body. Ed was able to listen in to the conversation via a microphone and the sessions were recorded with the client's knowledge. Sinbad had freshly shaved his scalp, put on his large gold hoop earrings, and a clean white shirt. I sat beside the desk, not behind it, as Ed had suggested. This was meant to put the client at ease, but what would put me at ease? Because this was a "get to know you session," we talked about his life before prison as well as his incarceration. He grew up in East Oakland with no father figure in the home and was a gang member by age twelve. He had been in and out of prison repeatedly. When I asked why he had been jailed the last time, he looked me straight in the eye and said, "I killed a guy in a fight. They got me for manslaughter."

"So you killed a man," I said in my best Rogerian manner.

"Well, they only caught me for that one," he replied. "I don't take no shit from nobody, Chump," he said, and he gave me a bump in the arm like we were street bros. We talked about his classes at the college and how he was managing to keep up. According to Sinbad the classes were easy and he really wanted to be on the college football team. I was surprised that a forty-two-year-old former inmate wanted to be on a Junior College football team. He told me the coach was a chump because he wanted Sinbad to be a lineman, while Sinbad wanted to be the quarterback or nothing. He would be nothing.

After Sinbad was released that fall, he was living in a half-way house in San Francisco while his rehab counselor explored job opportunities in the Bay Area. I had my radio on early one November morning and I couldn't believe my ears. It seemed a certain Carl Weston (aka Sinbad) had been arrested in downtown San Francisco after trying to extort money from United Airlines. He said he would blow up an airplane at SFO, if he didn't receive a hundred thousand dollars. He would pick up the money near a phone booth in the downtown business section of the city. The police showed up and so did Sinbad, not realizing that threatening an airliner isn't a wise thing to do, especially from a phone booth. Like I said, he was naïve. I wonder if he is hearing voices again in some faraway cell.

A few weeks later a client named Becky, a twenty-eight-year- old unmarried woman, was due to be released. She had been a model client, participated in group, was well groomed, and seemed poised for work on the outside. Two days before her release date she attempted suicide on the ward. She cut herself repeatedly with glass taken from a mirror. She was sent to the hospital medical ward, a full medical hospital within the grounds. She could handle the stress on the ward but not the threat of living on the outside. Unfortunately, this reaction is very common. Patients become "institutionalized," comfortable in a controlled environment, but unable to function outside of that setting. This happens not only in prisons and hospitals such as Napa, but also in universities, the military, and even marriages. Change is difficult to confront even for well-adjusted individuals.

It was getting near the end of my internship and I was now in the throes of a dilemma. I needed to put my life in order. First of all I had to find employment. I loved Colorado but knew that the job market there was poor. California was going through much the same financial meltdown. Ronald Regan was governor and he was beginning to close down the social welfare programs in the state; Vocational Rehab was one of these. Rehab was replacing counselors who retired or quit the service, but they were not creating any new positions. In order to qualify for these few jobs, candidates had to go before a review board of Rehab Directors as well as having the proper paper work in place. I had my transcripts sent to the State Department of Vocational Rehab. They assumed I would graduate on time in December, and I was scheduled for a placement interview.

One early December morning, I walked up to the Rehab Office in nearby Concord to confront my review panel. I thought I was adequately prepared. I was seated in front of two men and one woman representing the State Department of Voc. Rehab. The first questions were low ball. Why had I moved from New Hampshire? Why counseling? Why had I left Hawaii? Did I have family? And on it went until the woman in the panel question me at length about the Napa State program. "Did I think it was beneficial to the clients or would they better suited to be assigned to a counselor on the outside?" I praised the program because it was all I knew of California Rehab. She dug deeper into the kind of work we were doing and the expected outcomes. Did I know how many clients had been successfully placed in positions in the last year? I had no idea, but I put my best spin on it. When the hour long conference was finished, I thought I had performed well but was confused by the many questions about the Napa Hospital Program.

The staff back on B ward wanted to know how things went. I told them about the grilling I received from the woman on the panel. "Oh, no!" Ed said. "That was Betty Dotter, and she has tried to close our program repeatedly. She is a pariah to us and I'm afraid that you stepped into the middle of a bag of shit."

I had no idea that our program was on thin ice. As it turned out, I received an eighty-five score for the interview. I assumed that was like a B grade. It was, but that was a sub-par grade in a competitive market. I had been blindsided. I had only a few short weeks left on the ward. I had only one job interview scheduled in the Contra Costa County Office, but that job was offered to another candidate. That weekend I visited with my friend and classmate, Tom K., who was also in need of a position with the Department. He was also interviewed by the panel and was given a ninety-five. He and his lovely wife lived in the San Jose area. He said he had been offered a position at the state prison at Soledad but turned it down. A week later I was offered the same position. After visiting Canon City Penitentiary in Colorado, I could not see myself in a prison environment. I turned down the offer as well. Later in the same week, Tom reluctantly accepted the position. His wife was pregnant, and he needed the money. Two years later Tom left the Rehab Office at Soledad after a friend and fellow counselor was killed by an inmate. He later took a position as a counselor in an alcohol and drug rehabilitation center in Monterey.

My master's degree graduation was scheduled in Greeley the week before Christmas. I could not attend because I was still working on the Ward and needed to continue my job search. My diploma was mailed to me. My parents wanted to attend my graduation, but instead bought tickets to San Francisco for a weeklong visit. They were very dismayed to see my living conditions over the geriatric ward. I introduced them to the B Ward staff and their eyes were opened wide when they saw that the clients I worked with seemed perfectly normal, with a few exceptions. We visited Gary and Kathy in Daly City, went to the Napa wineries, toured San Francisco, and Reno. I was totally embarrassed when they insisted on bringing me to a show on North Beach featuring female impersonators. When I took them to SFO for the flight home, Mom cried and my Dad gave me two hundred dollars for a suit. I needed the money more than a suit.

I finished my internship on the Ward but had paid for the room until the end of the month, however, Ed, my supervisor, invited me to stay with him in Fairfax. His wife and I reluctantly agreed to this temporary arrangement. It was time to get serious about a job, any job. Nothing was happening with the Department of Voc. Rehab, so I also began looking for teaching positions. I interviewed for a post in Walnut Creek at a sheltered workshop for the disabled. It would neither be teaching nor counseling, but supervising work on the factory floor. The pay was very poor by Bay Area standards. Although I would be working with the disabled population, I would be using neither my education nor counseling degrees. I turned down the offer. I sent letters to all Bay Area Departments of Education and made numerous phone calls, hoping against hope that a position would turn up in the middle of the school year. I got a message on Ed's answering machine, a state of the art device at the time. The Oakland Public Unified School District wanted to talk to me.

CHAPTER 7

LOCKWOOD SCHOOL OAKLAND

I arrived for my interview at the huge downtown Oakland School offices a half hour early with sweating pits and high hopes. I was shown into an assistant superintendent's office. His bulk was almost equal in size to his desk. He stared at me for several moments until he said, "We really don't have any openings that I know of, but why do you want to work with the Oakland Unified School District?" I gave him my best spin. I had worked in Special Ed., worked with minorities in Hawaii, had experience in a State Hospital, my references were excellent, and I needed work. "I see that you don't have a California teaching credential," he stated as my heart sank, "but I'd like you to go down stairs and talk to Dr. T, our Director of Special Education." He smiled, said, "Good Luck" and shook my hand while he made a call to Dr. T.

I waited outside the Special Ed. Department for another half hour before being shown into the Director's office. I was greeted by two men, the director and the assistant director of Special Education. Again I was asked the usual questions, but they focused on my experience with minorities. I admitted that New Hampshire had few minorities, indeed there were no African Americans students in my high school and only a few at Keene State. However, I did have experience with Polynesian students and dealt with black and Hispanic clients at Napa State Hospital. They seemed somewhat impressed. I was excused and told to wait in the hall. In less than twenty minutes, I was called back. Only the assistant director greeted me and said, "You are in Luck. We have a psychologist who recently identified enough children to open a new class in one of our elementary schools. If your papers are in order, we can offer you the job." I was both thrilled and frightened but readily agreed to take the position. I was about to begin my career in Special Education that would carry me through the next thirty-one years.

My welcome at Ed Merrick's house had worn thin, and I needed to find my own lodging. The teaching position would begin right after the Christmas break, and I would have an income for the first time in a year and a half. San Francisco housing is among the most expensive in the nation, but I heard from some of our clients on the ward that there was a unique housing opportunity in San Francisco called Resident Clubs. These were rooms in former hotels or large homes that rented on a weekly basis. Rooms could be let either on a singular or shared basis. They provided breakfasts and dinners, except on Sundays. These residences were run like hotels, providing living space for students, temporary workers, and those who could not afford a rental in the city. This seemed like a reasonable way to proceed.

I found just such a Resident Club in the heart of the city on Larkin Street and moved in. Larkin St., between Clay and Sacramento Streets, was a great location. It was within walking distance to the Marina, Chinatown, and downtown. It was, however, close to the notorious Tenderloin and the quirky Polk Street. Polk Street was eye opening. It was where the more flamboyant gay crowd hung out. It featured gay night clubs, bath houses, and restaurants. A walk down Polk was an introduction to the theater of the weird.

I spent Christmas with a friend from Derry. John was in the Air Force and was stationed in San Bernardino. The drive south gave me an opportunity to see more this state I wanted to call home. When I returned Ed invited me to his home while Erika was away in Germany. As we sat by the fire watching TV, Ed pulled out an enormous joint. It was a Christmas gift from a friend and Ed wanted to share. I seldom smoked grass, but, hey, it was New Years. I still am not sure what was in that rolled paper, but it was powerful stuff and sounds and colors took on new dimensions. Erika maintained German traditions for Christmas. One of these was to have rich chocolate ornaments on the tree. Ed and I became fixated on the chocolate on the tree as the "munchies" kicked in. We attacked, and when finished, the carpet was littered with former ornaments. Poor Ed, Erika would not be pleased and I would not be there. On the way back to the city, I crossed the Golden Gate Bridge. It seemed to take a year and a half to get across the orange span. I have never been that wasted before or since. Luckily I found my way to Larkin Street and my bed.

My roommate at the Club was an architectural student at nearby Heald College. He was a pipe smoking, good natured, artist named Peter. He was a naval reserve officer, a California native, and was straight. Peter showed me around the city and introduced me to some friends, one of them from Boston. Others in the building included an opera singer, several actors who had roles in local plays, a few gay office workers, and many new residents to the city who, like myself, were trying to get their bearings in a new city. It was truly an eclectic group, and I enjoyed my stay there.

At breakfast one morning, Peter introduced me to the others at our table. "This is Gene, he just was released from Napa State Hospital," he said with tongue in cheek. A young woman sitting beside me lit up like a sixty watt bulb. "Really? What ward were you in? I was on A." Oops! What could I say, "Just kidding?" Like I said, a truly eclectic group.

New Year's Day was spent in silent panic, tomorrow I would be faced with fifteen smiling faces waiting to be told what to do. Where does one even begin? Oakland for the uninitiated, lies across the Bay Bridge from its big brother San Francisco and is bordered by Berkley on one side and San Leandro on the other. More than the bay separates San Francisco and Oakland. There are many fine neighborhoods in Oakland, indeed the Piedmont enclave which is surrounded by Oakland is one of the wealthiest in the Bay Area. The area south of the 580 freeway is anything but. East Oakland in 1971 was an area of inner city poverty and heavily minority. The Lockwood School neighborhood had one of the highest rates of homicide, poverty, and chronic health problems in the Bay Area.

Lockwood was an elementary school with an enrollment of over nine hundred students in kindergarten through sixth grade. Over ninety-five percent of the students and sixty-five percent of the staff were African-American. It sat on what was then East 14th Street and 66th Ave, not far from the Oakland Coliseum. Immediately behind the school, and separated by a twelve foot high chain-link fence, was Havenscourt Junior

High with over a thousand students enrolled. Many of the students came from the "projects," an area of low income government housing notorious for crime and despair. Lockwood had among its notables, Frank Robinson, baseball hall of famer; and Bobby Seal, founder of the Black Panthers. The school was seen by many of the children as a sheltering and nurturing refuge from their home life. It was January 2, 1971. Ready or not, here I came.

The main Lockwood building was a yellowing two-story concrete mass with an adjacent cafeteria. An all asphalt playground reflected the midday sun. There was no grass, except on the street side where students were forbidden, and there were no trees for shade. Resting on the asphalt were numerous portable classrooms, originally meant to be temporary, but were growing in number and becoming rundown. Among the portables were the four Special Ed. classrooms secluded against the back fence separating the two schools and isolated from the general school population.

I met the assistant director of Special Ed. in the school library on the second floor. As we waited for Lockwood's principal, a ruckus occurred on the street below. We watched as over one hundred Hell's Angels on Harleys roared past the school. "Must be another Angels funeral," Mr. Fern, the principal, said as I greeted my new boss. "You'll need to go downtown and fill out paperwork and we will see you tomorrow at 8:30 a.m." As I drove the five miles back to the Oakland Unified Main Building, I noted changing neighborhoods. Around East 14th and 66Th the store fronts had bars, the single story homes had locked gates, and there were no supermarkets, only convenience stores with overpriced junk food and low end liquors. The neighborhoods improved markedly as I drove toward downtown. I sensed then that Lockwood was going to be a special challenge.

The next morning I drove across the Bay Bridge, took the Nimitz Freeway, and turned left on Haganberger toward *my school.* Mr. Fern greeted me stiffly and introduced me to Levi Reeves. Levi, a forty-year-old African American man in a neat sports jacket and possessing a dignified air, shook my hand. He welcomed me not only to Lockwood but to the Special Education program. I spent my first day following Levi like a trusting poodle awaiting a handout. Levi's classroom was overcrowded with eager children from first through third grader. I was hired, in part, to relieve Levi of this overcrowding. My portable would be adjacent to Levi's. He was to become my role model, mentor, and friend. I helped him with class assignments, followed Levi on playground duty where I answer numerous "who you?" questions, and had lunch with many of the other seventy-five staff members. The final bell rang at 3:15, and there was a brief Special Ed. Staff meeting. There I was introduced to Mrs. Willy, a seemingly over-wrought middle-aged black woman, and Mr. Washington, a very dignified black man with gray hair and a controlled baritone voice that exuded control. I would be taking some of Mrs. Willy's children as well as Levi's along with several others who were recently identified. Tomorrow, my third salaried day, would finally begin with my own students.

I arrived early, went to the teachers' supply room, gathering supplies and courage. At 8:30 Levi escorted a line of six children into portable 12A, my new kingdom. The six were my early reading group, another five pupils would arrive at 9:15. They were in the late reading group and would leave at 3:15, forty-five minutes after the early group left. I enjoyed the split reading group. It allowed more individual help and instilled in the students a sense that reading was a priority in the classroom.

My students sat nervously as I introduced myself as Mr. Thibeault, not Mr. Genes as in Hawaii. "Now please take out your readers," I said with tenuous authority. After a labored reading session we had recess, where I had yard duty for the first time. I walked around the huge asphalt yard smiling at faces that looked back with curiosity, suspicion, and occasionally contempt. We reassembled in 12A, where I had five new faces awaiting me, bringing our class to eleven students. It was math time but first introductions.

My students entered and sat in chairs I had formed in a semi-circle. "Mr. T, what 'bout the flag?" I heard a soft voice stammer. Oh, right, I thought, flag salute. After the flag salute and attendance it was "Circle time." This circle time became a mainstay in my classroom throughout my career. Bright-eyed and handsome Sylvester jumped from his seat. "I be Sylvester, this be Paul, who be you?" I knew right then that Sylvester and his sidekick Paul were the pair I had to win over if I was to be the Alpha Dog in my classroom. The others included shy Sandra, with eyes as soft and distant as a coastal fog; Regina, always talking seldom listening; Chandra, overweight and belligerent; Ralph, Hispanic with poor English skills, and five others who blended into the background. I liked what I saw and knew I was in for an enjoyable journey. For now I had five girls and six boys. They were second and third graders, ages eight through ten and, although they were designated as EMR (educable mentally retarded), I saw no organic disabilities. In 1972 Special Ed. students were identified by IQ, poor performance in the regular class, and too often behavior issues. In later years most of these students would have the advantage of a Resource Room where they could get special help but would be with their peers in regular classes.

Levi warned me to be in control of the class first and foremost. I asked Sylvester if he liked Mr. Reeves. "Yeah, he be mean," he said with a challenge.

"How is he mean?"

"You don't be good, he slap you in the butt."

"No he doesn't," I replied.

"Yeah, he do, Miss Willey too." I heard from numerous voices.

I intended to talk to Levi about this. I decided not to correct grammar in the class but would use proper English myself as a role model. Later Oakland Schools would adapt Ebonics (African-American Vernacular) as a recognizable language. An idea that was very controversial and hotly debated. It was later dismissed. I would not tolerate swearing, however, or disrespectful language directed toward myself or my students. I hoped to have a classroom with energy and movement but with control. I wanted to make school fun and meaningful and become a safe home away from home. I demanded respect and would respect the students in return. How to gain that respect was the issue I had to deal with for the first few weeks of school.

When school was dismissed, I spoke to Levi about spanking. He told me that the home life of the students included spankings but too often beatings. He used spanking judiciously and with parental approval. As a white teacher of small black children, I had to find another way. Levi suggested, a time out area. I would try this but wasn't sure how to implement it. Would it be a desk, standing in the corner, or a sectioned off area? Would it even work? The second week I found a partial answer.

Paul was a slow-moving overweight boy of nine with low self-esteem. He had poor achievement in the regular class due more to his inability to focus than any innate learning disability. Unfortunately he looked up to his pal Sylvester for direction more than he did me. One morning after recess, Paul refused to finish his math paper and was becoming a disturbance to others. I asked him to cooperate and sit quietly. "You ain't my boss," he shot back with a snarl. "When you're in my classroom, I am," I replied.

"Screw you, you ain't," I heard him reply in an almost sub-vocal snarl. Time to test a timeout. "Paul you stand here in the corner until you can be quit."

"No I ain't gonna." We were at an impasse. I had put Paul in a tough spot, but he reluctantly moved to the corner. After a minute, he walked away. I put my hands on his shoulder and stood him back in the corner. His head went forward and he bit his lip. He ran out of the classroom shouting, "I'm getting my daddy, honkey." Paul ran across the playground and off the school grounds. Shit! I had blown it. Confrontations like this were not productive. I had lost my cool and maybe my control over the students, and it was just my second week.

We had no direct communication with the front office other than sending notes and I had no aide or adult volunteer, so I went next door to Levi for help. He looked at me wide-eyed, shook his head, and said, "Wheee, Paul's daddy is a Black Panther and sleeps during the day. He can get nasty, but I know him well and I'll leave my door open looking out for him, but you should handle this on your own." Talk about tough love. I gulped and went back to my anxious class. They were waiting to see how I would react. I continued as if nothing was amiss. Ten minutes later there was a knock on my door. I opened it and was staring at a mountain of a man with Paul smirking at me from behind his enraged father.

"What happened to my boys lip?" I heard in a deep, commanding voice. I explained as calmly as I could that Paul had disturbed the class, cussed me, and ran away from school after I stood him in the corner where he bit his lip. As I spoke I noticed Levi looking intently at the three of us from his stoop.

"Dat what happened, son?" Dad asked Paul.

Paul smiled and said, "Yeah, Daddy." His expression turned from confidence to terror when his dad said to me, "I'm taking Paul home now, and he won't bother you no more. If he do, you call me, Mr. T."

As Paul was escorted from 12A by his father, I glanced at Levi who smiled who gave me a thumbs up and a nod. Whew! I found out later that Paul's mother worked as a volunteer in the school library. I conferred with her often, much to Paul's consternation and we had a bond from then on. Paul and I had an understanding, and Sylvester was relegated to second in command. Paul wasn't happy but learned to live with my restrictions.

The faculty at Lockwood was divided more by age than by race. The younger staff was predominantly white and idealistic, the older faculty were mostly black and beaten down by the system. There were exceptions to be sure. I was drawn to a small host of teachers. We would often meet in the morning before school, shared coffee, stories, and ideas. Gerry was the comedian of the staff. He had wild hair on his face and head and was never without a colorful story. Gretchen, born and raised in Oakland, was our earth mother. She had a wonderful disposition and could find a comfort spot in the midst of chaos. Others included Margret, a beauty who was putting her husband through Berkley; Helen, an easy going San Franciscan; Bart, the head of the Oakland Federation of Teachers (the more militant of the two teacher organizations); and Bonnie, our very proficient math specialist. Two of the younger teachers were black, Paul with his ubiquitous bow tie was the best dressed teacher in the school (and most likely gay), and Charlene who had a smile that drove all the men wild (present company included). There had been racial tensions with the staff in the past, especially when Martin Luther King was assassinated, but I seldom witnessed any lingering conflicts. On Fridays the male staff wore Dashikis, the colorful long shirts worn in West Africa. The Black Panthers ran a breakfast program to ensure that all kids had adequate nutrition before class. Other Panthers were involved with the Parent Teachers Association.

Often after classes, especially on Fridays, the younger teachers would gather at the Mexicali Rose, a popular Mexican restaurant/bar near downtown. We would unwind with salsa, tacos, and margaritas. Thank God for the Mexicali Rose. It provided me a chance to share ideas and concerns with my peers, as well as damn good food and jokes. I felt a part of a dedicated group of idealists who faced a difficult task with humor.

Returning to my roommate and friends at the residence club, I would share my trials and tribulations. Weekends were spent finding new cheap San Francisco eats, walking the hills of Marin County, or visiting with Gary Phelan in the fog of Daly City. Mondays, however, it was back across the Bay Bridge to Lockwood and Room 12A.

Sylvester, hmm, how to handle this bundle of non-stop vigor. He was the energizer bunny on speed. He was very likeable, a nicely dressed handsome boy, whom everyone seemed to know and like. Attention deficit disorder was not recognized back in 1971, but I surely saw it in young Sylvester. He wasn't mean or purposely disruptive, he just couldn't stay focused. He was constantly off task. This, of course, made things difficult for the other children all of whom had their own issues. Gerry, my comedic friend, said,

"Send him to my room with a note when he needs to release some pent up energy, and I'll send one back." So I'd send a note saying, "See you at lunch?" Gerry would reply, "Not on my dime," and Sylvester would feel a sense of accomplishment. It worked. Sylvester, was my wingman in the class. Once he was in tune, he was an asset, a noisy one but reliable.

Lovely Sandra was an enigma. She was a tall, slim, eight-year-old who walked with her head bent toward the ground as if always afraid of making a mistake. I felt that she could handle the challenge of a regular class load, once I got her to thrive in my classroom. I was at a loss, however, as to a method. I realized that failure begets more failure and these children had seen enough of it. Sandra personified this culture of defeat. As I did back in Dublin, I did not mark paperwork with anything but positive reinforcement, maybe a happy face, a star, a sticker, or a "100%." Math was my vehicle for positive reinforcement. My children loved doing their math or pluses and take-aways, as they called it. I didn't have any math textbooks to follow, so each evening I would prepare mimeographs (an antiquated mode of preparing duplicate papers) for the class. There were always several different levels of difficulty, and I adjusted papers to individual performance. There was a subtle buzz in the room during math time, finger counting and raising hands when they were finished or had questions. I implemented number lines, pasting them on each child's desk. These were numbered zero through twenty and were about two feet long. "Three-plus-four meant placing a finger on three and taking four steps *forward*. A finger ends on seven and that is the answer. Subtraction; "7-3="—place a finger on seven and step *backward* three steps. The answer is four because that is where you stopped. I moved throughout the room constantly checking papers and going through the steps on student's number lines. I wanted to see papers that were one hundred percent correct. I think the kids loved math because it was the one aspect of their schooling where there was a solid answer. There were no shades of gray. We later even got into negative numbers using the number line. I never tried to have my students memorize their addition or subtraction combinations. These students don't deal in the abstract but eventually most knew the combinations by heart.

Reading is not as easily taught. I feel we read for two reasons; to gather information and for pure pleasure. Enjoyment in reading doesn't come from drills but from becoming involved in the story. I had textbooks available, but they were the usual Dick and Jane, ugh, with the typical white family; mother, father, Dick, Jane, Baby, and a dog named Spot. I was required to use these outdated books, but I thought I had a better idea. One, I had story time where I read to the class. Two, we used sentence lines where each student had vocabulary sight words they mastered on tag board. They would make up sentences using these words. Nouns and a few verbs to start, then progressing to adjectives and pronouns. A typical sentence may be. "My cat is Fluff"; progressing to "My cat Fluff is yellow and pretty," and on and on. When my class was busy, discipline was not a problem.

One morning I heard a knock on my door. When I opened it, there stood a man who would change my professional life. Before me stood Buzz Glass. He had been an Oakland School legend as a dance instructor, but was unknown to me. Buzz was the force behind a dance program that had been the pride of Oakland students for years. Budget considerations had put an end to dance in the district. Buzz could have retired, but he loved working with children. The downtown powers that be decided Buzz could best use his talents as a Special Education supervisor. He was, in a sense, my boss. Buzz stood just a bit over five feet, was Don Knotts thin, and in his mid-sixties. He looked at me from behind his thick glasses and after introducing himself, said, "Mr. Thibeault, can I do some fun things with your class." The next thirty minutes were magic. He put a vinyl disk on the record player and had the kids sitting in a circle. They performed a clapping exercise, then a circle dance, then a song. In short, he had my kids eating out of his hand. He was supposed to be supervising me, instead he taught me. He reinforced to me that movement is a wonderful tool, fun in the classroom is necessary, song and dance are constructive tools, and that teaching is performance. I loved Buzz!

That weekend I went to a pawn shop and bought an old guitar and a few song books. I had played very basic guitar while at Keene but was never very accomplished. Indeed, I was bad but I could strum and play chords. I practiced such standards, as "This Old Man," "If You're Happy and You Know it," "Coming Around the Mountain," etc... The next week at circle time we were rocking. We would invite Levi's class to join us as payback to him for mentoring me. When things got stale in the class I would take out the guitar and have the kids start moving. Now I needed a way to calm the class down when things got too loud and control was slipping from my grasp. I pulled a trick from my student teaching days. I would start counting from one to ten. When I reached ten the expectation was that the class would be in their seats with "hands down." "Hands down" meant students would be seated at their desks with hands down on the desk and eyes on me. This usually worked well. I could count quickly or slow to a crawl. There was the occasional "eight and a half, nine, nine and a half, pause, ten." Years later as a Dad, I would start a count and my daughter would say, "Stop counting, Dad." I never did get to ten with her and wasn't sure what I would do if I had.

Another trick I tried as the weather got warmer and the school year was beginning to wane was a token economy. I was having difficulty with my student's behavior toward each other and on the playground. There was too much pushing, yelling, and occasionally, outright aggression. I spent the weekend with construction paper making tokens. They were one-by-two inch colored pieces of construction paper the size of tickets. "What the hell are you doing?" asked my roommate, Peter. "Making tokens. You work you get paid. My kids work, they get paid." "But how can they spend these?" Good question! The following Monday morning when I found a student sitting quietly, I placed a token on his or her desk. Answer a question properly, get a token. Finish your paper work, get another token. When recess came. I asked, "Does

anyone have three tokens? You may be dismissed for recess."
The next students out had two, then one. "I want to go too,"
said Paul. "Do you have a token?" I asked. "No," he nearly
cried. "Well maybe you will get one after recess. You may go
out now." Luckily the kids bought into this program. I tried
never to take tickets away from them, just gave them
privileges bought with tokens. I had to modify the program
when I found that some children were swapping tokens while
on the playground for snacks, or even stealing them. It was
working too well. I had to collect tokens before dismissal and
put them into individual "ticket banks." By the end of the
year, I was having trouble keeping track of the numbers and
finding enough rewards. It was a good idea whose time had
come and gone.

In the spring of that year, I moved out of the Residence
Club and into an apartment on Twin Peaks. The one bedroom
flat was shared with Nancy whom I had met at the residence
club. Do the math. She was a petite Oklahoman with a lovely
smile. The arrangement was short-lived, however, and I
found myself living on top of the hill alone.

In the last month of my first year at Lockwood, it was
time for my annual evaluation with the principal, Mr. Fern. He
visited my classroom only one time and we were at circle
time then. I sat before him as he filled out my evaluation form.
He said, "I always give new teachers a *Fair* rating." I expected
something more from him, something constructive, or at least
a "good job." It never came, but I did get a contract for the
next school year. I had successfully made it through my first

year in East Oakland and was looking forward to next year. Mr. Fern retired at the end of the year.

That summer I found myself back in New Hampshire at Camp Wediko for the third and final time. I had outgrown the camp experience, but it gave me a little more income and gave my parents the false hope that I would return for good. I let the beard and hair grow long that summer. Hey it was 1971!

The summer flew by with few surprises and I found myself back in SF on Larkin Street in the residence club, luckily it was a short term stay. Within two weeks I found a roommate and we shared a two bedroom flat on Jackson Street in the upscale Pacific Heights neighborhood. My housemate was a thirty-year-old Bostonian, a would-be actor, and full time pain in the ass. He had no car and that proved to be our undoing, and the arrangement lasted only one month. I wasn't happy being a chauffeur, and his Irish temper surfaced far too often.

If I had no one to share the rent, it would be back to the residence club. I advertised in the roommate wanted section of the San Francisco Chronical stressing that I was straight. Shared flats in Pacific Heights were at a premium and within a week I met the ideal housemate. His name was John Harp, and he was the personification of a geek before geek was in. He had just moved to San Francisco from Seattle, was a software engineer working at a small new firm down the peninsular called Hewlett Packard. He often worked fourteen-hour days, so I had the flat to myself much of the time.

The 1971-72 school year proved to be an epic one for Oakland in general and Lockwood in particular. It began with a teacher work stoppage, aka, a strike. The more militant Oakland Federation of Teachers pushed for a work stoppage while the moderate Oakland Teacher Association wanted teachers to begin the school year on time, while only threatening to strike. The district wide joint teachers meeting was contentious at best. A vote was taken and teachers voted *not* to begin classes on time after Labor Day. I joined the picket line and was surprised to see my face on the evening news hiding behind the picket sign I carried in front of the Administration Building. It was a short two day strike but had lasting effects. The missing days were during the pre-school preparation. About seven in ten Lockwood teachers honored the work stoppage. Those who crossed the picket lines had to endure a school year of snide remarks and outright isolation in the teacher's lunch room. We gave a little and got a little from the strike action. I didn't feel it was worth the angst it caused.

Lockwood had a new Principal. Mr. Fern was replaced by a fiftyish-year-old black woman with the unlikely name of Mrs. Elvie Bible. She always wore a knit suit, glasses on a chain, seldom left her office, and became the subject of Gerry's non-stop humor. He always called her Elvie, but never to her face, of course. She left her office only when a photographer entered the campus. I don't think a photo at school was taken without her face sternly smiling in it.

The first few weeks of school were unbearably hot. The temps in Oakland were pushing one hundred degrees, and we had no air conditioning. My class made fans of construction paper, and I brought in an ice chest with bottled water. We had no plumbing in our portables. Tempers often flared as we stewed in our room. I lost mine a number of times as well. One day when the children were lining up after lunch recess, I slapped Sandra on the hand. She had been arguing with a classmate and well, I blew it. Sandra had an astonished look on her face, not that I hurt her physically, but she was shocked. I have seen many teachers spank pupils on the playground. I remember Mrs. Willy chasing a student with a book in hand and shouting, "Superintendent Marcus Forster approved this book, so I am going to spank you with it." I'm not sure she ever caught the offender or that the superintendent would approve of abusing his book. When we settled down in the classroom, I called Sandra aside. She was crying and afraid to talk to me. With her arms folded in front and her lips quivering, I apologized. "I shouldn't have slapped you, and it won't happen again. I am sorry, now you can take your seat." I wish I could say that I never slapped another student, but I did.

A new girl, Salina, came to me from Mr. Reeves' room. She was overweight and belligerent from the first day. She often cursed other students and me as well. One day out of frustration I gave her a smack in the behind. A small slap on the butt was normal among teachers at Lockwood, but it was not in my arsenal and I don't condone it. I felt badly then and still do to this day for my behavior toward Sandra and Salina. Sandra was forgiving, Salina was not. I was visited by Salina's mother the following day. She was infuriated. "I won't allow no white teacher to hit my child." Once more I apologized, but it fell on deaf ears. She headed to the office to see the principal, but she had to deal instead with the new vice principal, Levi Reeves. Levi, who had recently taken the job, calmed the mother. He had been Salina's teacher for two years and knew both mother and child. To settle things Salina was moved into Mrs. Willy's class. I wasn't sorry to see her go. You can't love all the children in your classroom, no matter how hard you try. Maybe Mrs. Willy could use an approved book to discipline Salina.

During the first month of classes, I had a visit from Levi Reeves. "Mr. Thibeault, I'd like to introduce you to Mr. and Mrs. Lee, and this is their daughter Ann." Ann Lee would be with me for as long as I was at Lockwood, much to her consternation. She was the first of my children who had obvious physical etiology. She was the only Asian student in the school which led in part to her aloofness. She was tiny with thick glasses and rarely spoke beyond a whisper and even that had to be pulled from her. Ann would not willingly participate in activities including music time and rhythm games. Her overly-concerned parents tried hard to involve Ann in her schoolwork. Mrs. Lee often sat in to our classroom, but even then Ann would not come out of her shell. Ann just distrusted me plain and simple. One Sunday, I was shopping in San Francisco's Chinatown, when from behind a food stand who should I see, but the Lees with Ann in tow. She looked at me in horror, as if I had been stalking her. Poor Ann, I guess I was her worst nightmare and here I was in her world, Chinatown. I'm not sure she ever got over that chance encounter. I did find a way to get through to her eventually. I had another shy girl, Shelia, and I teamed her with Ann. This arrangement helped both of them. In future years, I used peer tutors, but Shelia and Ann were my first pair.

One afternoon, the Lockwood members of Oakland Federation of Teachers were meeting in a portable adjacent to the street. Most of the younger faculty were present. Bart G was the school representative. If there was a militant teacher at Lockwood, Bart was the man. He was dressed in his usual fatigue jacket. Bart lived in Berkeley and drove past "People's Park" each day occasionally smelling of tear gas when he arrived in school. Just as the meeting was wrapping up, something flew through the open door. There was an incredibly loud explosion and we all dove for the floor. Part of the wooden floor was splintered and Margie was bleeding. We all had ringing in our ears as smoke enveloped the small room. We rushed outside in time to see two teenagers running across the playground. They had thrown two cherry bombs into our meeting. In a confined space these now outlawed devices can cause a lot of damage. We never found out who threw them but in all likely hood they came from the nearby Junior High. Nobody was seriously injured, but we were all shaken by the incident.

I occasionally heard footsteps on the roof of 12A. Havenscourt students would climb the chain-link fence, sit on my portable, and smoke, sometimes cigarettes and sometimes stronger stuff. If left my class to shoo them away, I would be greeted with insults and pelted with lit butts, before they sauntered to their side of the fence. Our lone campus security was Levi and as vice principal he had better luck chasing them. Eventually the Havenscourt Security patrolled the portables and helped alleviate the situation.

Once the hot September was over, I settled into the routine of class. I introduced Cuisenaire Rods for math with limited results. These are color coded sticks, each one centimeter longer than the other. By manipulating those students could perform various math functions. Like a number line, they are a multisensory approach to math. I used whatever method worked best for the individual. Music and circle time is something that the whole class seemed to embrace. Even Sylvester and Paul bought into the routines, reluctantly participated, and even enjoyed the activities. Buzz Glass visited often and we were able to share ideas about how to involve children in rhythms and dance. These activities could advance academic goals, by counting beats, rhyming words, and using basic vocabulary words. We often invited other classes to join us, socializing with children outside of the classroom was important and my kids loved to perform.

Gerry would usually share his dittos with me when we met at the ditto machine before school. He provided coloring papers, follow the dot sheets, and simple puzzles. The week the machine broke down Gerry had withdrawal symptoms. He said ditto fluid ran in his veins and he often slept with dreams of dittos in his shaggy head. We had to invent new activities for a solid week. Oh, the heartache.

Unfortunately, real tragedy struck our campus later that fall. One morning before school a lone man with a handgun walked from the street, across the playground, and into

Margie's portable. In front of several students, he held a gun to Margie's head while he raped her. He was never found and arrested as far as I know. We were in shock! Margie was taken to the hospital, treated, and never returned to the classroom. The lack of security at the school had finally ended in disaster. Many of us had often visited Margie's class before school for gossip and coffee. Had one of us been there, the rape may not have happened, or the rapist may have turned the gun on a visitor. The teacher's lounge was a sober room for months. Even though we worked in a troubled community, the school seemed to be a refuge from the troubled streets. That was no longer true.

Sandra in her shy way was often the source of wonderment to me. One morning, she came into the classroom before school. She couldn't wait to tell me a story. "Mr. T, last night dis honkey, he come into the projects," she started. "Nobody knows why, but my mommy, she said I best stay away from them Honkies. They don't belong near these apartments." Sandra's story went on repeating her mother's mistrust in white men visiting in her neighborhood. When finished, Sandra looked at me with incredulity in her eyes. "Mr. T, you ain't white, is you?"

I just laughed. "Yes Sandra, I am."

"Well you ain't like that," she shot back. It was time for a race lesson for both of us. We weren't black or white, we were just people who cared for, and respected each other.

I once walked my class to the local library which was only a block from school. On a street corner stood a gang of young men drinking from bottles wrapped in paper bags. They stopped talking and gawked at this white guy walking ten black children, one Asian girl, and a Hispanic boy through their neighborhood. Sandra noted their stares, looked at me, and said, "They must think you're our daddy." I had to love Sandra.

After school and on weekends, I was enjoying my life in San Francisco. John my, flat mate, and I got along really well. I took a rock climbing course with the Sierra Club, bought a rope, a harness, and talked John into joining me on the cliffs near the beaches in Marin. We would even string my climbing rope around the stairs of our flat and ascend or would stem in the small alley between our home and the neighbor's. We were even talking about writing a book, <u>First Ascents of 2950 Jackson Street</u> but thought our landlord would not be pleased. John's girlfriend, Duffy was spending more and more time in our flat and she was a joy to be around. She caught me by surprise one day as I exited the bathroom before fully zipping up. I was embarrassed, but Duffy just smiled and said, "Don't worry, if I see anything I don't recognize I'll ask questions."

John came home one day bursting with pride. He showed me a six-by-eight inch machine. He purchased it from the company where he worked for only two hundred dollars. It was the first time I had ever seen an electronic calculator. I was very impressed. John and Duffy were two of the most intelligent friends I have ever known. John wrote software for one the first cardiac scanning machines, and Duffy worked at Stanford Medical pioneering in nuclear medicine. What a pair, and I was teaching them how to climb rocks. Go figure.

That fall I volunteered to work for San Francisco Suicide Prevention. I wanted to put my counseling education to some use. After a few weeks manning phones with experienced personnel, I was assigned a partner, Mindy. She was a tall blonde from Arizona who worked as an editor for a travel magazine. I was blown away by her professional demeanor, her striking looks, and her unforgettable smile. We worked four hour shifts three days a month and once a month we worked an "all-nighter," eleven p.m. to six a.m. San Francisco was often called the suicide capital of the nation, a reputation it didn't deserve. I think the Golden Gate Bridge drew would-be jumpers from other areas. Most of the calls were routine. Most callers were lonely, mentally impaired, or enjoyed crank calling. We kept records of frequent callers, but took first names only. Typically I'd recognize someone and occasionally callers would ask for specific volunteers. Mindy got too many crank calls with suggestive or explicit language. We were able to listen in to each other's lines when we put callers on speaker. We would also pass notes to each other. Most nights were routine and on "all-nighters," we could usually get some sleep taking turns on a roll-a-way bed near the phones.

One night I had a male caller who was very distraught. He had just broken up with his girlfriend, saw no point in going on, and called to tell someone why he was killing himself. "I've got my gun right here, and you are going to hear the shot. I just needed to tell *someone* goodbye," he stuttered. The noise on the line certainly sounded like he had a revolver. I threw a note to Mindy. It read, "Get a trace on line one and call the police." Meanwhile, I tried to talk the caller down and attempted to control of my heart which felt about to leave my chest. I tried to stall by calmly asking personal questions. "Do you have family in the city? Are you from here? Missouri? I've been there." And so it went but he easily saw through this stalling technique yet he did not hang up. Mindy returned a note about ten minutes later. It read, "I got an address, police on the way, keep him talking." The caller suddenly became much more agitated, "You f*cker, you called the cops. They're outside, I'm going to kill a few of them first, then myself." Another note to Mindy, "He is armed and is threatening to shoot the police." He dropped the phone and I heard banging on the door, a scuffle, and a new voice on the line. "We got him." Click! That was it, no thank you, no good work? Mindy and I just hugged, both shaken from the experience, but thankful that things turned out well. Just another all-nighter at Suicide Prevention.

Mindy and I became good friends. My Ford Falcone finally gave up the ghost and I bought a new Chevy Vega. It was orange. Another chick magnet! Mindy was my first passenger. We headed north of Mount Tam and down route 1 along the coast. She loved hearing stories of my teaching, and I loved being with Mindy. I picked her up one night for dinner and her roommate (also a stunner) introduced me to her date. He was none other than RC Owens, former all-pro receiver with the 49ers. He shared a drink with me but appeared to be thinking, "What is Mindy doing with this long-haired loser?" Mindy always kept things platonic and even tried to fix me up with one of her best friends, Mickey. Mickey and I dated a few times, but nothing clicked for either of us. We usually talked about Mindy.

Christmas vacation was spent with my former roommate, Peter, in Utah and Colorado, skiing but soon it was back to Lockwood. It was time for my semiannual evaluation from Mrs. Bible. As soon as she entered the room I pulled out the guitar and we serenaded her with a rousing chorus of "She'll be Coming 'round the Mountain." She beamed and left saying nice work Mr. "Theebolt." Hmm, I snowed her but, she doesn't even know my name. Thank God for Buzz Glass.

I dumped the token economy in favor of charts with stars. Instead of passing out tokens, I placed stars on a chart near a student's name and hung the chart in front of the room. Five red stars equals a silver star, five silvers equals a gold, and so it went. The kids bought into it. Even Ann beamed when she earned stars. I gave out rewards when they reached a certain level. I bought small toys and knick-knacks in Chinatown and passed them out as rewards. I finally achieved good control of my classroom environment. This became apparent one morning when the class was particularly noisy. I sat at my desk and didn't say a word. I had a copy of the SF Chronical that I opened and pretended to read. The kids stopped their talking and looked at me for clues. I gave them none, just kept reading the newspaper and not smiling. Soon they were all seating quietly at the desks with "hands down." After three long minutes of silence, I put down the paper. "Now" I said, "we may be ready for class."

My reading groups were still split with an a.m. and a p.m. grouping. One warm spring afternoon during reading I suddenly realized that all the students were laughing at me. I had fallen asleep, in middle of the thirty-fourth reading of a book. I must have had an all-nighter at suicide prevention. I often allowed the children a five or ten minute quite time after lunch recess. They would have their heads on their desks or were allowed to lie down on the rug. Often there would be napping at this time but that was the first afternoon that I took a nap.

That spring Frank Robinson, manager of the Baltimore Orioles, visited the school. His sister worked in the office and he made an effort to visit his old school whenever the Orioles played the Oakland As. Once or twice in the spring we would take a field trip and walk to the Oakland Coliseum and, if lucky, we could see the Athletics at practice when we met a kindly security guard. It was only a peek, but my boys loved seeing Reggie Jackson or Rollie Fingers in the flesh. We could then follow the team and use the experience for reading or math projects.

Something amazing happened to my special Sandra in the spring of '72. She was always a reluctant reader and struggled to learn sight words. Over the course of a few weeks, Sandra's reading began to blossom. I don't know why or how but she clicked on reading. She went through three years of reading primers in three months. I just kept feeding her books. She would sit quietly reading and occasionally ask me for help with a word. I gave her extra time in the library to choose books. If she asked to read during math, I let her read. Her mother and I decided that she should try regular class and come to me for extra help if necessary. She spent the last month in regular second grade and was holding her own. She would start the fall sessions in third grade. I must admit that she never should have been deposited in Special Ed. in the first place. Unfortunately, once a child is identified as EMR it is very difficult to reverse the decision. Thankfully, things have changed since then.

The summer of 1972 was spent in Europe. I saved for that trip the entire year. I had a backpack, a Eur-rail Pass, and a Europe On Ten-Dollars-a-Day guide. What more would one need? I had sixty-five days off, and I spent sixty-two of them on the trip. Thirteen countries later, I arrived back in Oakland, hair and beard longer and a lot worldlier. I reconnected with Milo my Irish pal from Camp Wediko. Not to my surprise, I found he was a member of the IRA. I spent a week with him and four other members on a trip to the North of Ireland, then hitched back to Belfast, never talking politics with the drivers. It was after all, the time of the "troubles." I also hooked up with my flat mate, John's old girlfriend, a nurse from Denmark. The trip was a revelation and sparked a love of travel that I have yet to satiate.

The 72-73 school year would be one of transition both personally and professionally. I was still sharing a flat with John H. and occasionally his squeeze Duffy. I became good friends with Gerry, Gretchen, and her husband, Randy. I often stayed in Oakland after school to join Randy and Gerry in a game of basketball. I continued to work with Mindy at Suicide Prevention and frequented the Abby Tavern with Peter from the residence club. I picked up a habit of a Guinness or two on Friday nights, I loved Ireland. We also frequently visited a local comedy club, the Holy City Zoo, where we would laugh till we cried at this new young comic named Robin Williams.

Life in 12A was going well. I had a few new students and said goodbye to some favorites as well. Sylvester and Paul moved on, but would often visit me before classes began. Like many of the staff, I used my own money to shop at a teacher's supply store. Our supply budgets had been severely limited. Class was still fun and the neighborhood still depressing. One morning when I was in a hurry, I left my briefcase on the roof of my car. It had been parked on a side street near the playground. I didn't realize my error until lunchtime. I rushed to the car knowing my papers would be gone. Not at all. It remained just as I left it. I asked myself, would that be the case in my high-end San Francisco neighborhood?

Two new teachers joined in our lunchroom conversations, where we debated world affairs, school politics, and Mrs. Bible's wardrobe. They were a young married white couple, Liz and Paul. Like the rest of us they were full of idealism and enthusiasm. Liz taught second grade, and Paul taught sixth. Paul had played football at Cal and still had the build of an NFL linebacker. One lunch hour he joined our group and was very distraught. He actually cried and said, "I can't go back in there. These kids won't listen and they are learning nothing." We all fired him up with stories of how we overcame the same problems. "Go back in there like you did in a big game and kick some butt," we told him. By the time we finished with our pep talk, he was fully charged. We could hear him all over the play yard. "I said, quiet and line up NOW." I smiled as I piloted my charges into our room, knowing Paul would be alright.

Real tragedy found its way into the Oakland Public Schools in November. Marcus Foster, Oakland's superintendent, was brought to Oakland in 1970 from Philadelphia where he was a nationally renowned educator. He was hired to revamp Oakland failing schools. As he left his office one evening he was assassinated in the parking lot before reaching his car. A radical group called the Symbionese Liberation Army (SLA) claimed credit. The Oakland community was in shock and security became a priority. Once again the nation's attention turned toward Oakland's troubled schools.

The mood at Lockwood was sober, even the children seemed subdued. No one knew about the SLA, or what they stood for. On February 4, 1973 the SLA became nationally known when they broke into a Berkeley apartment. They kidnaped newspaper heiress Patty Hearst, thus beginning a two year headline grabbing odyssey that would end in Hearst being sought for her participation in a bank robbery in Sacramento. Each morning that spring, I unknowingly drove by the San Francisco house where she was held. The SLA demanded that Hearst's wealthy father, the son of William Randolph Hearst, provide free food for the poor of Oakland. During a school open house most parents told me that they would not accept any food from these terrorists. I was proud of their attitude. They would not accept a handout even though they could use it. Others in the neighborhood were not so principled. I saw the food truck distributing groceries and lines of families accepting "blood food."

Work at Suicide Prevention continued, and I still partnered with Mindy. We often referred callers to the emergency room at SF General for psychological help. One Saturday evening Mindy and I decide to see exactly where we were sending them. We sat in the emergency waiting room from 10 p.m. until 12 a.m. Patients without obvious life threatening trauma had to sit in plastic chairs, wait for hours for a dose of medication, and watch gunshot or traffic victims being wheeled by. This was not a place to send callers with psychological problems, and we no longer did so routinely.

One evening Mindy and I went out for dinner at Fisherman's Warf. She left her apartment in a hurry and grabbed a letter as we departed. At dinner she opened it. The look on her face was one of pure devastation. Her lips were quivering, she turned pale, and tears ran down her cheeks. "My God, what is it?" I asked.

She just said, "We have to leave." We did so without ordering. "Let's go to the beach and talk," she cried. I drove to Baker Beach, a narrow strip of sand below the Presidio and the Golden Gate Bridge. We walked arm in arm. She told me of her recent week in Hawaii. She had met a Navy pilot whom she considered her soul mate. The mystery letter was from his mother. His plane had been shot down over Vietnam. He was missing in action and presumed killed. Gulp! We walked, talked, sat in the sand, talked, walked, sat, talked, cried, and walked as the hours passed by. I took Mindy to her apartment as the sun was rising over the Oakland Hills. I had school that day but just went through the motions. I had such ambivalent feelings. I had hoped that we would be more than good friends, yet I empathized with her grief. We both lost something that night. We would never be that close again. Mindy became obsessed in the belief that her pilot was still alive and that they would be together again. He was never found to the best of my knowledge.

One day at lunch Levi entered the lunch room looking down hearted and perplexed. "What's up Levi," said our matronly school psychologist. Levi sighed and said, "I just caught a six grade boy and girl in the boy's bathroom and they were going at it hot and heavy. Can you imagine at their age?" Our kindly gray-haired psychologist looked at Levi with compassion and said, "Oh well, it's Friday."

Our lunch room conversation was dominated by the SLA, Watergate, and the fabulous sweet potato pie that the school cooks made. On the playground, one of my more quiet students, Isabell, was talking to a classmate about her mother's loathing of hippies, a not uncommon attitude in the black community. Hard working poor families or mothers feel hippies are rich lazy slackers. Isabell looked at me and said, "Mr. T, are you a hippy?"

I laughed, "No Izzy, I am not a hippy." That evening I looked in the mirror at my beard, long hair, and casual dress, thinking parents of my students couldn't be blamed for mistaking me for a beat character. Maybe a haircut was in the near future. I could also lose some weight. A run or two wouldn't hurt.

In April, John and Duffy decided to live together closer to Stanford. I had to find a new roommate or find another living arrangement. My first San Francisco roommate, Peter, had room available in his huge flat in the avenues. I was able to move in with four other bachelors. I felt that I was back in the fraternity house. Each of us had our own room and shared in the cooking and cleaning up. Some shared more than others and the cooking was at best edible and sometimes digestible. I joined the Sierra Singles; an outing club for singles with ties to the Sierra Club. We went cross country skiing in the Sierras, hiking in Marin, and getting together socially. On a canoe trip to the Russian River North of the city, I shared a ride with a new member of the club, Wendy. Her phone voice was earthy and warm. We met, shared a ride on the river, dumped the canoe once or twice, and had a great time. We met again for dinner later that week, then again and again. She was athletic, intelligent, and we were having fun together. She worked for IBM. I met with her fellow IBMers and felt like a duck out of water. They wore suits, ties, and white shirts. I, on the other hand, well enough said. I was driving to New Hampshire once again for the summer, but Wendy and I decided to meet in Colorado at her father's home and then drive back to San Francisco together.

School was winding down and was going well. On the playground, however, I was still just that Special Ed. teacher. One afternoon as I was leaving, there was a crowd of junior high students gathered on the playground. A black female teacher, Pam, was trying to break up a fight and was having no luck. I had to help. I pushed through the crowd and stood between the two fighters, who both outweighed me. There were lots of shouts of "Leave them alone," and "Fair fight, butt out." I said, "Take it off the school property, now!" Surprisingly they did, but not without lots of cursing. As I watched them exit the yard, Pam shook my quivering hand and offered thanks.

There was a knock on my door one afternoon. It was Buzz Glass and an older woman whom he introduced as Mary Brantley. Dr. Brantley was a psychologist and the director of Low Incident Special Services. She made me an offer that I could not refuse. A new class for the Multiply Handicapped (MH) was opening up next fall. She offered me the position with a recommendation from Buzz. I would be changing schools, would have fewer children, have an aide, and be teaching children who were truly "Special Needs" kids. I jumped at the opportunity.

During my last week at Lockwood there was an assembly. Mrs. Bible, still in her knit suit, presented end of the year awards for students. At the end of her presentation she gave gifts for retiring teachers and staff who were leaving the school. The last person called to the stage was "Mr. Thebolt." Two years and she still didn't know my name. I was given a plastic ballpoint pen with Lockwood engraved in the school colors, a sickly yellow and green. Later that afternoon with colleagues at the Mexicali Rose, I stomped on the pen among cheers and tequila. That is how I left Lockwood. I really did enjoy the experience. It was not always easy, but I met good and dedicated people. I would miss the children but was ready to move on. Interestingly, most of the younger teachers with whom I worked would also leave the school eventually. Gretchen moved to a small town in the Sierra Nevada Foothills, and Gerry bought a Birkenstock shoe store where he could joke with customers to his heart's content.

CHAPTER 8

FRUITVALE MULTI-HANDICAPPED

Summer in New Hampshire was spent leisurely. I took several weeks driving through Western Canada, across the plains of Alberta, Saskatchewan, Manitoba, and into the deep forests of Ontario and the Northern US. At times New England seemed like a foreign world to me, with its ancient hills and dark woods. I was able to reconnect with friends and family after three years of living in California. Once more Ben Low traveled west with me. We met Wendy in Loveland Colorado at her Father's home. We spent an interesting night camping on the Colorado River near Moab in a canyon called Negro Bill. After dark, the vertical red walls were suddenly lit as if God himself were present. I hadn't realized that tourist boats prowled the river at night illuminating the canyon walls with huge spotlights. Later that night, we were disturbed by lights of another kind and voices that seemed threatening. Two fully loaded Jeeps had pulled in and were questioning why anyone would be camping where they had chosen to party. After a good scare, they moved on down the canyon. Early in the morning the skies opened with a downpour complete with thunder, very nearby lightening, and an amazing rainbow. As if by magic, waterfalls emerged from the canyon walls. We counted a dozen or more and the bottom of the once dry wash began to flash flood. As we 'rapidly packed up and left we saw the Jeeps hightailing it out in front of the raising waters.

Once back in San Francisco, Wendy and I moved in together, first into her apartment, then into a flat next to Golden Gate Park and the University of San Francisco. A November San Francisco wedding was planned. It was a truly an eclectic wedding. It took place in a Swedenborgian church, the best man was Jewish, the maid of honor a fundamentalist Christian, me sort of Catholic, Wendy agnostic. Wendy's mother insisted on a formal wedding and reception. Wendy's stepdad paid the bill. The whole affair was overwhelming. I knew few of the invited guests other than my former roommates and my parents. They came from New Hampshire and were wined and dined in the City by the Bay. After the reception Wendy and I drove through pouring rain to Santa Cruz and collapsed, grateful to escape the crowd.

Fruitvale School was to be my new home away from home. Unlike Lockwood, Fruitvale had a racially mixed enrollment. In fact a friend's kindergarten class had nine different first languages. How anyone teaches in this environment is beyond me. The enrollment was half that of Lockwood and there was no Junior High next door. Once again I was in a portable in back of the main building, but this time, I had direct communication with the office and the assistance of a classroom aide. Her name was Erica. She was a young, very regimented East German immigrant with a severe disposition. When I heard her story I gave her more slack. She had escaped from East Germany in the trunk of a car, married an American serviceman, and moved to the Bay Area. We had to establish a working relationship that benefited the children and allowed Erica some leeway. It would be a project.

At the faculty meeting the day before school began, I sat toward the back of the faculty room. The school's new Principal, Mrs. Gardner, called to me saying, "Mr. Thibeault (pronounced correctly) you and I are both new here so why don't you sit up front with me." So much for sinking into the background as I did at Lockwood. Mildred Gardner was an attractive black woman in her thirties. She was tall, poised, and put people at ease with her charm. She was a hands-on administrator who was both respected and loved by the school community. I felt welcomed by the new staff. Like the community, the staff was a mix of white, Hispanic, and black.

My new MH class was initially limited to just six students and was the only special class in the school. I had the benefit of a TV, a classroom sink, and luckily the service of Buzz Glass. My students included Michael and Jeffery, two white ten year olds who lived together in a foster home. They had obvious physical and cognitive impairments. Michael was a tall and lean, while Jeffery was short and squat. Joseph was a small charming black boy with a winning smile but strange behavior. He, too, was a foster child with a penchant for finding used chewing gum, a habit that needed changing. Andrea was a thin shy black girl with limited speech, but personal charm. Sherri was an eleven-year-old white girl with cerebral palsy and emotional struggles. Then there was Ronnell. He was a handsome African American boy with a violent temperament. He would be my project this year, and I would be his tormentor.

My children definitely stood out on the playground. I insisted, initially, that either Erika or I would be on the playground with them. I needed to protect them from teasing but eventually wanted to wean them from our protection. Most of the children at Fruitvale had not been exposed to others with disabilities. I wanted to slowly integrate my students into the general population. Recess breaks and lunch were learning opportunities and I wanted my children to be included. The other teachers were supportive, but I no longer had the close relationships I did at Lockwood and I missed them dearly. The idealism and sense of purpose I saw among the younger teachers at Lockwood was not apparent with the older Fruitvale staff.

All of my students came to school by bus and none lived in the immediate neighborhood. I had little parent involvement as most of the children were in foster care, Ronnell was the exception. His mother was a single parent and Ronnell was her only child. She drove a bus for the district and watched over her son like a hawk. Joseph was the smallest and sweetest of my youngsters. He was so innocent and trusting of everyone that he had to be taught appropriate social skills for his own safety. Sherri had violent temper tantrums that were best ignored whenever possible. I felt her outbursts were reinforced at home by honoring her demands. Michael and Jeffery were like two peas in a pod. They were both were low functioning and easily frustrated. I would have to work at giving them positive encouragement. Andrea would like to hide from school if she could, but she had expressive eyes that spoke when she could not. Language skills were her most pressing need. I tried to let Erika know how I wished each child to be treated. After a month, she came around to my way of running the classroom.

I continued to have a circle time first thing in the morning and used the guitar and rhythms to enhance language and social skills. Most formal skills required one-on-one teaching. I often had Erika watching over others as I introduced tasks to individuals. Sesame Street was frequently on at this time. Ronnell had the most going for himself academically. He knew basic math, some limited reading, and could print fairly neatly. He was, however, way below his grade level. At the best of times, I had Ronnell help Michael and Jeffery with paperwork which helped with his self-esteem. Academically little Joseph tried so very hard. He had been reading in a pre-primer book for a month or more and seemed to be advancing when I mistakenly turned two pages and he parroted the missed page. He had memorized the entire book using pictures for clues but was not actually reading the words. He had snowed me. Andrea, Michael, and Jeffery had limited abilities, but could manage reading their names, street addresses, phone numbers, and other important personal information. They were able to count and add using number lines. I spent an inordinate amount of time teaching clock skills and then someone with more sense than me invented the digital clock. I found the same to be true with shoe tying. Where was Velcro when I started teaching? Unfortunately Sherri had few academic skills, and I had little success when I attempted teaching those to her. Life is not on a piece of paper. Socializing and language would be my goals for her.

I was able, occasionally, to reserve a station wagon for local field trips. I took the children out into the community as much as possible. We once had a trip to Lake Merritt Park near downtown Oakland. Most of my kids seldom visited public areas in their own city. Lake Merritt had nature trails and, as the name implies, a large lake. We would feed the ducks and geese, but in reality I was trying to have the children act appropriately in a public setting. As we left the lake for the car, Sherri became agitated and threw a doozy of a temper tantrum. She was down on the ground, with feet in the air, and proceeded to scream like she was being tortured. From past experience, I knew the best action in this case was no action at all. I slowly moved my class about fifteen yards away from the outburst but kept my eye on Sherri the whole time. Suddenly a very large black man appeared and picked up the bawling Sherri in his arms as if she were a rag doll. I rushed to confront him and as I did he tightened his grip on Sherri and gave me a look that only Jeffery Dahmer deserved. He would not put Sherri down until I had Erika bring the rest of the class toward him. As we walked to the car Sherri acted as if nothing had happened, while her rescuer just glowered at me. I had escaped a beating once again thanks to a small group of special needs children and an East German immigrant.

Ronnell was not happy to be included in a class with students who were so obviously impaired. He sought other friends while on the playground but was often bullied. His reaction was to act out. Cursing, spitting, and sometimes outright fighting was common with Ronnell. In the late fall a new student was assigned to my class. His name was David, who like Ronnell, was a normal looking black boy but could not function in a normal class environment. He had some academic skills and, when not under pressure, functioned well in my more sheltered room. He and Ronnell became good buddies, leaving Ronnell not feeling so isolated. One lunch recess, I was observing my students on the playground through my classroom window. A small group on boys were harassing some of my children. This small gang was led by a large boy who was particularly abusive. I watched unseen as David confronted the leader. David suddenly reared back and let go with a right cross that connected. The bully sprawled on the asphalt, and David walked away. I smiled to myself and never spoke of this to anyone. David had taken on the Goliath of playground and won. Things went more smoothly on the recess yard after that.

I attended a PE workshop put on by none other than Buzz Glass and a cohort of his named Jack Capon. Jack Capon was a local educator and developer of "Perceptual Motor Activities" for young children. Jack and Buzz laid the ground work for my teaching of basic motor skills. I ordered all his records, books, and worksheets. These included basic motor activities in a developmental order such as balance, rhythms, eye-hand coordination, and other sensory motor skills. All of the children, no matter what developmental stage, could participate. I became a firm believer then, and still am, that motor skills should be taught at the earliest levels. Unfortunately, few elementary schools put an emphasis on basic movement skills. Too often PE is a recess with twenty or more children and two balls. Doesn't leave much ball time for those who need it most, does it?

Wendy and I enjoyed our apartment near Golden Gate Park. The huge park is a great wooded escape in the middle of San Francisco. I had put on considerable weight and vowed to start jogging. My goal was to run the length of the park from our home to its end at the Pacific Ocean, and walk back. I had watched the famous Bay to Breakers Race and was inspired. In the early seventies the race had a few hundred entrants. By the mid-eighties the numbers were approaching seventy-five *thousand*. I managed to do the three downhill miles to the beach but soon quit running. Just too much work. I still played some basketball with Gerry and Randy thinking that was enough exercise.

The first year at Fruitvale went quickly. David went on to another program, much to Ronnell's frustration. Ronnell and I had our disagreements and a few times I had to physically hold him from behind while telling him I will let go of one arm when it is under control, then the next arm, then a full release. We would next discuss what happened and how to avoid tantrums. This is the technique I learned at Camp Wediko for the emotionally disturbed and it had worked well there. I wished that Ronnell could have been a Wediko camper. He would have learned so much. In spite of his flare ups, he let go of some barriers and saw me as a father figure. During the short time I worked with him, I saw real emotional growth.

I was still young and impatient with the lack of progress from my students. Michael in particular. He had such a great attitude but often he would completely forget overnight what had taken him a week to learn. In frustration I once threw his reading book on the floor. "Michael, you know those words, damn it!" Erika then took over as I regained some composure. Poor Mike, I was hard on him and always felt regret afterwards. Friends often say, "You teach Special Ed. You must be very patient." Not true, not even close.

I assumed that classroom pets were calming so I had a small cage in which we kept a pair of mice, unfortunately they were not the same sex. Soon two mice begat eight. The kids were charmed. I became alarmed. The mice were breeding like, well, mice. Soon we were overrun with the little rodents. Luckily one of the fifth grade teachers was raising a snake in his class and I found a solution to the mice hordes. None of my children discovered my devious resolution to our mice overpopulation. Some of my students could add, but none could multiply. Thank God. Once again, Erika was horrified.

In spite of limited equipment I tried to teach some cooking, cleaning, and social interactions. I bought a hot plate to make pudding, oatmeal, hot chocolate, and the like. I often would ask, "What did you have for super last night?" Joseph would usually say, "Oh, just some beans and rice." The other children had a bit more variety but not much. Ronnell again was the exception. He was always well-dressed and well fed. My foster children were living on limited budgets, but there was no excuse for Joseph's poor and boring diet. I'm sure at home chips and sodas were a mainstay for some. Fruitvale had no hot breakfast program provided by the Black Panthers as we had at Lockwood. No wonder Joseph tried to get all the gum he could off the playground. I tended to bring in the occasional fruit and nut treats for the children to offset the junk food.

The year flew by. Christmas had us on stage more as a walk on than an integral part of the school program, but at least we were part of the school's social activities. I was surprised when Ronnell's mother gave me a Christmas gift, a pair of socks. It was the first gift I'd received since I had mangos given to me in Nanakuli.

In the spring, we took a field trip to a famous "all you can eat buffet" in nearby San Leandro. My bosses, Mary Brantley and Mrs. Gardner, approved the trip as a socialization activity. I liked the free lunch. The children were amazed, but none more than little Joseph. "Mr. T, what can I have?" I answered, "Whatever you want, but you have to eat all that you take and save some room for desert." Joseph's eye grew wider than a 747 as he headed to the serving tables. I saw a sixty pound boy demolish three plates of food, before desert. There was no bottom in Joseph. He put neither beans nor rice on his plate. Erika and I shook our heads in disbelief. It was one of Joseph's happiest moments in his young life. Even Sherri's behavior was appropriate and all the class had a great day.

The spring turned to summer and once again I signed a contract for the next year with the same school, same room, same class, and mostly the same children. Wendy and I hiked in Yosemite, enjoyed the city, and otherwise spent a relaxed summer in San Francisco. We even talked about purchasing a home and starting a family.

At Fruitvale, I was relieved that Sherrie took her temper tantrums to another district. Her foster mother had run out of patience. Richie, a new boy with cerebral palsy and subsequent learning defects, became friendly with volatile Ronnell. I teamed them together for seat work as often as I could. Ronnell seemed to relish the "Big Brother" role. Andrea and Joseph continued to make slow progress. Both seemed to have grown during the summer. Michael and Jeffery remained with me as well. We would add Angela and Tim during the year. They fit in well after some initial training. Each Friday in the fall, school classes were released an hour early because the neighboring field held high school football games. In Oakland, night football games were deemed too dangerous. There had been many fights and gang activity, therefore games were held Friday afternoons. I often stayed to watch the games and marveled at the athletic skill of these teams. Thinking back to my high school days, we wouldn't belong on the same field as the weakest of Oakland City High Schools.

In the beginning of October, I was very excited because I had tickets to the three World Series games that were to be played in Oakland. It was the Athletics against the hated LA Dodges. They had split the first two games in LA. The As were going for three straight World Series wins. That hadn't been done since the Yankee's in the Fifties. The day before the first game, I was having lunch in my classroom when I suddenly felt violently ill with a knife like pain penetrating my left side. After ten minutes, I felt much better as the children were entering the class. Erika took one look at me and said, "Get to the office." "No, I'm okay," I argued just as the pain hit again. I stumbled across the playground and into the office. Mrs. Gardner saw me and asked if I wanted and ambulance. I said, "Just let me lie down." I went into the infirmary laid down and ten minutes later was screaming in pain. Jose, our music teacher, held my hand and tried to get me to relax while Mrs. Gardner did call the ambulance. When EMTs arrived, I insisted on walking out of school, not wanting students to see me on a gurney. I remember the blaring of the siren, the awful pain, and a shot of morphine. X-rays confirmed a kidney stone, my first but, unfortunately, not my last. Mrs. Gardner arrived just in time to see me vomit over my hospital gown. Oh, the humility. Wendy arrived along with Randy Johnson and Gretchen shortly after I was admitted to my hospital room. I reluctantly handed Randy that day and the next day's World Series tickets. I was forced to watch on television. I stayed at Kaiser for two days and begged to be let out on Friday the day of the last game. Reluctantly the doctors agreed. I was let out at noon and headed directly to the Coliseum arriving in time for the game. Not only did Oakland win the game but won the series four games to one over the detested Dodges. I was ready for class on Monday.

In October, I used some of my field trip budget to take the children to San Francisco and the Grand National Rodeo. It was held annually since 1941 at the Cow Palace. We attended in the morning which was just a horse show with various venders selling cowboy paraphernalia. The kids were well-behaved, ate cotton candy, drank sodas, and loved seeing the livestock (I know, I gave them junk food). Before heading for the car and the trip back to Oakland, I took our boys to the men's room while Erika took the girls to theirs. My boys were all lined up at the urinals with their pants around their ankles, when a large older gentleman entered and stood at the urinal next to little Joseph. He was dressed in very expensive western wear, hat, boots and all. I saw Joseph's eyes open wide as he turned toward the gentleman. Joseph, with wonder in his voice asked, "Are you a real cowboy?" Unfortunately for the man, Joseph had not finished his business. I withheld a laugh as Joseph peed on a five hundred dollar pair of boots. I rushed my gang out of the restroom as fast as I could and never looked back. Joseph was totally unaware of his faux pas.

Later in the fall, we had our annual back to school night. Erika was quite good at preparing the bulletin board and art projects so our room looked really nice. Each child had his or her best papers on their desks. Unfortunately, I only had Ronnell's mother as a visitor. She was pleased with his progress. He was doing much better at school, and it carried over to the home. The foster parents did not show. Their kids were fed and clothed but not given the nurturing they required. In the case of Joseph, he was hardly fed. That night our custodian was watching over the staff and visitor's cars on the playground. After most of the parents had returned home, he was approached by a gang and beaten severely. Once more, there was violence in Oakland Schools.

I had playground duty one afternoon when I witnessed a fourth grade boy harassing Michael and Jeffery. I didn't know his name but recognized him as a playground bully who had often abused my children. I asked for his name and room number. "F*ck you, retarded teacher," he screamed. I held him by the wrist and took him into the office. I explained exactly what happened to Mr. Gardner. She thanked me and let me know the child would be dealt with. This was far from his first outburst. I rushed back to comfort Michael and Jeffery. I kept a cautious eye from my portable during recesses after that. Three days later, Mrs. Gardner called me into her office. She said the boy who had bullied my children told his grandmother, who was raising him, that I had pulled on his arm and hurt him. Grammy had threatened me. She was an older black women in a wheelchair and was known to carry a gun hidden beneath her shawl. Mrs. Gardner had my back, absolved me of any wrong behavior, and counseled Grammy. For the rest of the year I rushed in and out of school, but I had no more problems with that bully or his Grandmother. It was refreshing to have an administrator stand up for a teacher and not just for the parent.

In the spring that year, I was once more approached by Mary Brantley with a new proposition. Children with the diagnosis of autism were a growing concern and the State of California was initiating programs to teach these children in regular public schools. Oakland would be among the first in the nation to start classes. Did I want to teach one? Well, yeah!

My class would still be at Fruitvale. Instructors from UC Santa Cruz would provide a week of training and then follow ups throughout the year. We would start with as few as two children and would have no more than six. Mary asked if I wished to keep Erika as my aide. I said, "I think she should stay with my old class for continuity." I broke the news to Erika in that manner and she accepted the reasoning, but not without rolling her eyes.

Wendy was pregnant, and we were expecting in late November. Our rental in San Francisco was not fit for a family, so we began looking to buy. San Francisco was just too expensive, thus we looked across the bay and found a lovely house in of all places, Oakland. It was in a very nice neighborhood, close to Lake Merritt, with bus service to San Francisco. We closed the deal for forty-two thousand and would have to live with a mortgage that was not much more than our rent. It needed a bit of work, orange walls and a green rug just didn't cut it for us. My summer was spent painting, putting in a bathroom in our basement with hopes of renting, and cycling on my new bike. We would be closer to our friends from Lockwood, Gerry and his new wife Pat, and Gretchen and Randy. The weather in Oakland was wonderful and about twenty degrees warmer than San Francisco's glacial summers. All in all, it was a very good move. By the time school began in late August, we had settled into our new home. I had an easier commute as did Wendy. It was quicker to get to her office in downtown SF from Oakland that to fight SF traffic in the city.

CHAPTER 9

AUTISTIC CLASS FRUITVALE

I knew little about Autism in 1975, but neither did the majority of the American public. I read literature by Bruno Bettelhiem which attributed Autism to poor parenting and cold uncaring mothers. These theories have, thankfully, been totally discredited. The main symptoms of Autism include poor social interaction, poor language development, and poor or unusual sensory development. There was no single diagnostic description of the condition. We had to observe a number of symptoms that were within the spectrum. It was, therefore, difficult to classify the children for inclusion in my class. I would just have to deal with each child on an individual basis with his or her own set of specific learning disabilities, really not much different than what I had been doing for the last few years.

The instructors from UC Santa Cruz had but one week of training for us before school began. So much to learn in such a short time. They suggested that we have little visual distraction in the classroom in order to avoid over-stimulating the students. Many autistic children have poor sensory figure-ground perception. We were to stand behind a student while instruction was given so that the child would pay attention to the task and not to clues in the teachers face. Language would be a major focus with the children, but we had no access to a language therapist. Emphasis was placed on a behavioral model. Find a reward meaningful to the child, be it food, praise, or some other "hook" and utilize behavior modification techniques. One on one instruction would be necessary. We were given training manuals and would have visitations from time to time by staff from UC Santa Cruz.

At Fruitvale, I prepared my room by having learning stations, which were essentially, three-sided cardboard boxes on top of a student's desk meant to avoid outside stimulus. The day before school, I met my new aide. Carmen was a young Hispanic women with a saucy ponytail, a winning smile, and bright brown eyes that seemed to emphasize her gentleness. I felt an immediate sense that she would be a great partner. She was willing to learn, to cooperate, and had empathy for the children. I had hit the jackpot with Carmen. My old class was next door and a Mrs. Wilton was hired to replace me. She was an older woman, had taught regular class, was returning to the classroom after raising her own children and had little experience with children with special needs. Although kindly, she seemed ill prepared to handle a multiple handicapped class. Erika was guiding her and was being heavy-handed with her need for control. Not my problem, I thought. I told Mrs. Wilton I would help whenever I could.

The first day of classes, I was surprised that I had only two children. Angela was so shy she just melted into a desk with her head down. She was eight, had been in Special Ed., but failed to flourish. Angela hummed quietly to herself to relieve her anxiety. From my limited experience with autistic children she did not seem to fit my expectations. Kevin, my other student, however, did. He was a small dark-skinned boy with a swivel head. He poked into every corner of the room. Kevin had limited vocalization but would suddenly shout whatever came into his mind. "Winston taste good," he yelled. Carmen and I just looked at each other and shook our heads. While Kevin was bouncing off the walls, Angela sat humming. Oh, boy, here we go. I grabbed Kevin, Carmen held onto Angela, and we walked around the school to familiarize them to their surroundings. Mrs. Gardner saw us and welcomed the children to the school. Kevin although hyperactive was compliant. He actually clung to me like a baby koala to its mom. He was fine as long as he was moving. Angela needed to be dragged along but seemed instantly to connect with Carmen.

Having just two children in a class didn't please one of the first grade teachers. During the first week, she it took upon herself to write letters to the Oakland Superintendent, the State Superintendent of Public Instruction, and the Governor; complaining about my lack of students. Someone got the message and within a week, I had a full class of six, several of whom should not have been diagnosed as autistic. It took me the remainder of the year to sort out those appropriately placed from those who were not. Gee, and I never got to thank her.

One morning during the first week, Mary Brantley knocked on my door accompanied by a young mother and a small boy. As they entered my room, the eight-year-old whirlwind ran through the classroom opening every cabinet and drawer, throwing all the contents on the floor. His distraught mother barred the door so he could not escape. He had no language, but let out a loud *burrrrrrrrr*, as he ran over the desks and destroyed my classroom. Mary had been trying to convince the parents that a placement in a public school would not be appropriate because we couldn't provide for his safety. The mother asked, "Where are your bathrooms?"

I replied, "They are in the main building." Mom saw that this situation would not meet her child's needs. I agreed whole heartedly. He needed more than I could provide, and he was not enrolled.

The children were transported to school by taxi, picked up at their homes and dropped off at school, hopefully fifteen minutes after the regular school began. Carmen met the children at the drop off point. One morning toward the beginning of the school year, Carmen came in giggling loudly. "What," I asked.

Through laughter she said, "The taxi driver just asked me if I was sure these kids could draw."

"Why?" Carmen asked him.

"Well," he replied, "Aren't they in an artistic class?" We needed to do some training with the drivers.

Boys outnumber girls with autism about four to one, however, I had three of each in my now full class. Angela was joined by Christine and Nancy; and Kevin with Robert and James. The children ranged from eight to ten years of age; three black, two white, one Hispanic; all had some verbal skills, but limited academic or social abilities.

One morning Kevin didn't get off the bus with the others. Instead, he was brought in by his mother. She was about thirty, a frail woman, with weary eyes. She was a single mother, worked in a medical office, and looked worn out. Life seemed to overwhelm her. She wanted to meet me and see where Kevin was spending his day. Kevin was excited to have his mom in the room. He took her to his cubical (desk), then to Carmen, the TV, and finally me. "What's wrong with my Kevin?" she asked with a soft timid voice. I tried to explain what I knew of the syndrome and assure her that Kevin was in good hands. Apparently she had never been informed about Kevin's autism but had just accepted what professionals told her. "Kevin, he so sweet", she pleaded. I could only agree and told her not to worry about labels. I let her know that we would do the best we could for Kevin and treat him with loving care. She shook my hand and left, hopefully feeling better about Kevin's placement. I wish I could have referred her for community help, but I didn't have the resources at my disposal. I gave her my home phone number and told her to call at any time. She seldom did. I visited Kevin's home one afternoon and saw that Kevin's mother kept a small, but tidy, house. Kevin raced around showing me everything in it. "Look, Thibeault, look."

My class of six was in a state of flux. Christine left after a few weeks. She was a foster child and typically had moved from home to home; this was especially true with impaired children. Carmen and I got along really well. She was intuitive and didn't need constant direction. She was also kind and passionate about the children. I couldn't ask for more. I no longer had the help of Buzz Glass, but Mary Brantley was only a phone call away.

November was fast approaching when Wendy and I were expecting our new daughter. We had been going to Lamaze classes and had prepare a nursery. Wendy left work a few weeks before the expected birth date. On November nineteenth, I received a message from the office to call home immediately. The time had come. I left school and drove the three miles to home reluctantly driving the speed limit. Wendy was packed and ready to go. Her water had broken, and we headed for Kaiser Hospital which was only a few minutes away. The labor was painful, but we were well prepared. Wendy was brave and shortly after midnight we had our little girl, Dawn Marie. We were expecting her to be born early in the morning, thus her name. If we stuck to that design she would have been named, Midnight Marie. We stuck with Dawn. I stayed at the hospital making sure both Wendy and Dawn were doing well, then headed for home. During the whole procedure, I felt emotionally strong. I, of course, was at the birth and was actually the first to see our daughter. I took the next school day off and headed back to Kaiser with a new Teddy Bear. I had the radio blasting away and was singing along, then Don Mclean began singing, "Wonderful Baby." Boom! I was hit with an emotional bomb. As tears of joy and wonderment poured out of me, I had to pull over to stop the deluge. Even now that song brings tears as I think back on that wonderful day. Our lives were about to change in a big way.

In early December, our class along with about eight hundred other students strolled into the Oakland Symphony Hall for a production of the Nutcracker. I went with a lot of trepidation, not knowing how my children would react to the noise, the crowd, and the disruption of routine. During the "Waltz of the Snowflakes," Kevin jumped up shouting, "Gasoline." He then sat as if nothing had happened. There were a few snickers but, looking around, I was sure no one knew where the sound came from. I put my arm around Kevin, reassured him, and we left with no further outbursts. God, I loved Kevin. Unlike many autistic children Kevin was not emotionally aloof; he clung to me. His eyes followed me continually for behavioral clues. When he became excited he would yell, "Thibeault" and point to what he saw or wanted. He had speech, but for the most part he was echoing, (echolalia) thus he repeated TV commercials. "Where's the Beef," he would shout completely out of the blue.

I sought a new approach with Kevin's language. Speech is transient. A vocal sentence is there and gone in an instant. Kevin seemed to understand speech, but couldn't decode the output. It all happened too fast. Reading, however, allows time to decode and encode words. He knew a number of sight words, so I started with "yes" and "no" written on his desk. If I asked a question, Kevin would point to the word and shout, "yes" or "no." This procedure evolved into Kevin putting together simple sentences using word cards. He would arrange, "I want (fill in the noun)," and then say the words out loud. He was so excited when he could communicate with others. His vocabulary increased slowly, but steadily. We labeled classroom items for him to identify verbally and his mom did the same at home. He was beginning to develop real language. He would, however, only verbalize with Mom,

Carmen, or me. My hope is that this skill will generalize, and he would be able to communicate with others appropriately.

During Christmas break, we packed Dawn and drove my Volkswagen bus to Colorado to spend the holidays with Wendy's dad and stepmom. On the long journey home and in the middle of nowhere, the VW stopped without warning. I flagged down a passing family car and sent Wendy and the baby to the nearest town, Vernal, Utah. I waited in the car. The temp was well below zero before a tow truck arrived and transported me and the VW thirty miles into town. We found a cheap motel room for the night. Vernal, Utah doesn't see many VWs, but a frustrated mechanic got the bus running again, kind of. We headed west through Utah on mountainous highway 40. The bus spit and snorted slowly up the hills but coasted down more easily. After lumbering along we reached Heber City, Utah. I thought, what a pretty town, but it is in the middle of nowhere. We surprisingly found a VW mechanic, who had the bus ready to go in less than two hours. He said, "The Vernal mechanic put Chevy points in the rotor." He fixed a torn gasket, filled the crankcase with oil, and charged us twenty-eight bucks. I could have kissed him. We made the trip back to Oakland with no further delays. Little did I know that forty years later I would call the Heber Valley my home. It took me all those years, but I found the same mechanic still putting cars together in the same garage. I thanked him again, withheld the kiss, but shook his hand.

I returned to a school after the holidays to shocking news. Mrs. Gardner was being reassigned. The entire community was up in arms, feeling that after years of failure they at last had a principal in whom they could believe. They felt betrayed. A committee of teachers, parents, and community leaders was formed to seek answers. The teachers chose me as one of two faculty representatives and the committee chose me as chairman. I was in over my head. The superintendent made the decision to remove Mrs. Gardner, so it was to her that we would have to address our issues. Dr. Ruth Love had been chosen to replace Marcus Foster after he was murdered by the SLA. She was a powerful black women who was not to be trifled with. She directed the national "Write to Read Program" and later became the controversial superintendent of Chicago Public Schools. We were told to deal with her deputy who was nothing more than a bureaucratic mouthpiece. He informed us that Mrs. Gardner was gone, but we could choose from an approved list of ten eligible candidates for the principal position. We, as a committee, would select three candidates after we interviewed and screened all ten. Dr. Love would then pick one of the three for the position. We worked quickly, but it took time and effort. We did find three educators, one of whom we felt would make an excellent replacement for Mrs. Gardner, and two who we could live with. These three were submitted to Dr. Love. A week later, notice came from Dr. Love's office that she had rejected all three of our choices. We, as a community, were incensed. At an evening meeting of the entire Fruitvale community, it was decided that we should approach Dr. Love personally to protest her decision. I, unfortunately, was the spokesman, but I felt that everyone had my back. The very next day I called Dr. Love's office only to be told that she was unavailable. I informed her secretary that two ministers from the community were ready to go and take our concerns to the media. She said she would let Dr. Love know of our grievance. Twenty minutes later, I received a call from Dr. Love's office and was put on hold. I had answered the phone while in the bathroom sitting on the throne and there I waited as Dr. Love came on the phone. "Of course, Mr. Thibeault, I would love to meet with your committee. How about on Monday after school?" She was so sweet as if she was always available to meet with us. Monday afternoon fifteen of us crowded into her lavish office. I presented our concerns. We loved Mrs. Gardner but realized that she was not an option we had. We had carefully screened and selected our choices and felt our time was wasted. Dr. Love listened carefully and smiling said she understood our concerns but as the final judge she could not approve our selections. Everyone in the room was mesmerized by Dr. Love's power and backed down leaving me to look like a hot head for questioning the brilliant boss of the Oakland schools. I felt that any chance I would ever have of an administration position in the district was lost. Dr. Love got the principal she wanted from the start, and we would have to live with her decision. Our new principal was a lot more of a Mrs. Bible than a Mrs. Gardner. Luckily, she treated me with deference knowing that I was the chair of the committee that had previously rejected her application.

One morning Mary Brantley once again entered my room with news of a new student to replace Christine. Her name was Judy. She was again a foster child and was seriously self-abusive. Mary said the child had this last chance in public schools, otherwise Child Services was about to send her to a custodial facility. She asked what I thought. I said, "Bring her in. I have room." Judy arrived the next day. She stepped into the classroom and immediately began hammering herself on the side of the head with a closed fists. POW, POW, POW! She had calluses on her cheeks from her self-destructive pummeling. In the past she had ruptured her ear drums and broken her nose. Her foster mom sent splints to cover her elbows so she could not hit herself. Why she didn't arrive with them on, I don't know. Judy just screamed for the first hour and then curled into a ball like a small hedgehog. She remained that way for the rest of the day. Judy was a very thin white girl of ten. She had stringy, almost white hair, long, thin features, and was nearly nonverbal. She seemed haunted and frightened by internal demons. Judy spent the first week screaming, "No" and little else. Still, there was something about Judy that was endearing.

After a while, Judy settled into a routine. She would arrive by cab without the splints, but had her arms tied down. Carmen would meet her and place the splints we made on Judy's thin arms and together they would walk to my room, hang up her coat, and take a seat. I used rewards for most of my children. I had crackers, popcorn, toys, etc... Judy would sweep any of these off her table and shout "no." I had no "hook" with Judy. Until one day we were playing with balloons, using them to bat into the air, and catching them. Judy was fascinated with the activity. When we popped them all, Judy look stunned. She tugged my arm and said in her scratchy voice, "balloon?" Gotch Ya! Judy would work for balloons. My goal was to rid her of those arm splints. They limited her in many ways. She knew hitting herself was not allowed, but couldn't control this deviant behavior. At times Judy surprised me with her caring for the others in the class. Angela had a crying session one day and Judy ran to me saying, "crying, Angela." In spite of all her limitations she showed compassion for others. I began limiting the size of her splints as well as her time in them. Within a few weeks, the cardboard rolls we used as splints went from twelve inches to three. At the taxi drop-off, Carmen would not put the splints on. Judy had to walk across the playground, hang up her things, take a seat, and say hello to me before splinting. In a month's time, I had reduced the cardboard to a small cloth ribbon, which I called psychological splints, because they didn't actually restrict her physically. Yet if I removed them, she would pummel herself. One morning I told Carmen, "Let's try giving Judy a test today, no damn splints." "Okay," Carmen said, "but we will have to keep on her all day." Judy sat in her seat and saw no cloth bands, her hands started toward her face. "No hitting," Carmen and I both said. Her hand only touched her face softly as if testing her self-control. Throughout the day we kept up this routine. She rubbed her face, maybe patted her face, but did not hit. Success! Now we could work on other behaviors, such as speech, social skills, and some word recognition.

We went on two field trips that spring. One to a children's play day in San Francisco's Golden Gate Park. Over three thousand children were in attendance. There were stage performances, face painting, balloon tricks (Judy loved this), and free food. I was taking care of Angela's running nose and when I turned around, Kevin was gone! He just disappeared. Carmen had the other five kids find a seat as I headed to find Kevin. He was still nonverbal outside of the classroom. I looked and saw a sea of faces, most of them black. I spent ten minutes walking around the grounds in a near panic when out of nowhere I heard, "Thibeault!" Kevin had found me! His grip on me was so tight, I thought he would never let go. Carmen and I knew we had dodged a bullet.

Our other memorable trip was a helicopter ride. We left from the Oakland Airport, flew to SFO, Berkeley, Marin County, and back to Oakland. This was a commuter air ride with special rates for children. I had parent approval as well as that of the powers that be downtown. The children saw their world differently and were so excited they could hardly contain themselves. Angela was the only one to seem overly concerned. She screamed when we took off each time but had a mile-wide smile the rest of the trip. I had to bite my lip when at a Special Ed. meeting Mary Brantley commented that some teacher actually took *her* class on a helicopter ride. Oops!

Carmen informed me that she was pregnant. I was happy for her and her husband. She would make a wonderful mother, but I would miss her in the classroom next year. One day at lunch recess as I was walking back to my room, I saw Carmen trying to take away a jump rope from a student. The boy had his back to me, and I saw him attempt to kick Carmen. I ran to intervene. It was Ronnell. I had worked so hard with him for two years on temper control but had seen his behavior regress under his new lenient teacher. I took him into my room for a talk. He began to fight me. I held him from behind as I had done when I was his teacher. He was totally out of control, so as I held him I told him I would release him when I saw him calming down. He spit, tried to bite, and cursed me. "You ain't my damn teacher. You can't tell me nothing," he continued. He did slowly get hold of his emotions, and I took him back to his room and his teacher. In the struggle his shirt had torn.

Within one week, I had a formal complaint filed against me by Ronnell's mother. She claimed I had roughed up her son, ripped his clothing, and cursed him. The incident was to be investigated by an administrator from the downtown office. To my relief I knew Mr. Roberts, the administrator who would question me. I filled out a report on the incident and met Mr. Roberts in his office. He looked bored. Apparently Ronnell's mother had filed reports several times before he had been in my class. Mr. Roberts told me not to worry about it and that as far as he was concerned I had done the right thing. I left his office with a sense of relief. Ronnell would not even look at me for remainder of the school year. I felt badly about the incident. I may have handled it poorly but was glad it ended as it did.

As the year wound to its end, Wendy and I talked about moving from the Bay Area. Although I enjoyed working for Oakland Schools, I did not want Dawn to attend them. I had seen violence, poor teaching, and overcrowding. The Bay Area is expensive, we had a poor babysitter for Dawn, and Wendy was tired of the commute. That summer I applied for work in several rural districts including the North Coast, the Sierra Foothills, and even a position in British Columbia. To my great surprise, I was offered a position in Prince George, BC. I had only a week to accept or decline the offer. Wendy and I had vacationed in BC, but not as far north as Prince George. I headed to the Oakland Public Library for information on this northern city. Prince George was far from ski areas, was a lumber town with pulp mills, had a large Native community, and brutal winters. I declined the offer.

The Mendocino County Schools could offer me only a summer school position, and I heard nothing from Placer or El Dorado schools. As July began to move on, I made a call to Bruce Becker the Director of Special Ed. in the foothill community of Auburn. I had applied for an advertised position, but had heard nothing from them. Bruce said he would like me to come to Auburn for an interview, although my application had been initially rejected. Bruce liked my experience so I got the invite. I made the two hour drive to Auburn and left feeling confident after my interview. Two weeks later, Bruce called saying he was sorry, but another applicant was chosen. He left me saying, "We liked you and if something comes up, we will be in touch." With that he hung up. Oh well, I thought, another year in Oakland. Two weeks later he did call back. "We have a teacher who just informed us that she is pregnant and her job is open, we would love to have you work for us." Wendy and I could not pass up the offer. I accepted. I was to work for the Placer County Office of Education for twenty-six years.

CHAPTER 10

PINE VIEW SCHOOL

Wendy and I had less than three weeks before school began. We had to sell a house, find another, move everything we owned, and prepare for a new lifestyle. We put our Oakland home up for sale and within a week we had a reasonable offer. The market was very hot in good Oakland neighborhoods and in one year we made almost twenty thousand dollars. Sold! The position I interviewed for was in Truckee, a railroad town near Lake Tahoe which often has the lowest temperatures in the US. The job I secured was in the small town of Newcastle, only five miles west of the county seat of Auburn in the California Gold Country. This was the area where the forty-niners settled in search of gold. The Sutter's Mill gold discovery site was only twelve miles south of Auburn. The American River runs a thousand feet below town and flows into Folsom Lake, then to the Sacramento River, the delta, and empties into San Francisco Bay. Wendy and I found a home in a small gated community called *Lake of the Pines*. It was twelve miles north of Auburn. The house was new and priced close to our Oakland home's selling point. These Sierra foothill towns are 1500 to 2000 feet in elevation which is above the valley fog and below the Sierra snow. An ideal place to raise our daughter.

The Placer County Office of Education (PCOE) operated two small schools in Newcastle, the PH School for the physically disabled and Pine View for the mentally disabled.

Pine View had five classrooms. Mine would house the older children; ages about nine to eleven. After leaving Pine View, children would move to classrooms at a facility that was housed in a former hospital. Our supervisor, Jack, had his office in the school for the PH children. He was pretty much a low key coordinator and we saw very little of him. I was the only male teacher in the school. Two classes were for the severally impaired; many of whom were in beds and needed total care. The other three were for the more moderately impaired; most of whom were verbal, and socially confident. My class was one of those. We had a small playground behind the school with grass and colorful playground equipment. The red brick one-story building was set up well for our population. It had a kitchen, laundry, adequate bathrooms, and spacious classrooms. The setting was rural, white, and middle class, a contrast to Oakland. The feeling was not unlike my little school in Dublin, NH.

I left Wendy and Dawn in Oakland to attend the teacher orientation where I met a friendly welcoming staff. My aide would be Jane Harwood, a fortyish woman who had been with the same group of children for years. Jane was small, energetic, and sure of herself, but seemed unsure of me. I was, after all, a male from the big city. I didn't consider myself Jane's boss, but rather a working partner. I would welcome her experience but needed to set my own agenda. We sometimes played good cop, bad cop with the children and Jane could handle either role. She also knew the parents and was a great help in that regard.

I slept the first two nights on a mattress in our new home with the smell of new paint and clean fresh dirt. I slept soundly listening to crickets chirping. I drove back to Oakland after the meeting on Friday. We packed on Saturday, moved on Sunday, and I began teaching on Monday. Two staff members lived nearby; Howard, a speech therapist, and Jim a teacher of the older moderately mentally impaired. They offered to help me unload and in the years to follow became fast friends.

Monday morning, Jane met the children as they nervously disembarked from the buses. All were transported by bus as none lived in Newcastle. The county provided classes and services for disabled students. Buses picked the students up at home and delivered them to school, door to door. My class would have about twelve children but I had only ten on my attendance sheet. When they arrived, Jane took them in, sat them in a circle, and we had introductions. During the five years I worked with this population, I would be known as "T-bow." It seems "Mister Thibeault" was just too much for them to spit out. I didn't mind at all. Some teachers went by first names and others by last names. Not sure why, it just worked out that way. One teacher was Jim and another Roskelly. My class was typical of the special populations that I trained with back in Keene. Half the class was composed of children with Down syndrome, the remainder had another types of organic impairments, some diagnosed, some not. I had two Davids, both with Down. They were like brothers. They had been together since preschool and knew each other's wants and needs better than I ever did. They were known as David A.

and David B. Steven was a slim boy with a generous stutter and a sweet trusting disposition. Mary was a high-functioning Down girl whose parents were very watchful and distrusting of the new male teacher. There was Bobbie, a Down girl whose father was a police chief in a neighboring town, and Heather a tall girl with moderate Cerebral Palsy. She walked with crutches and was fairly mobile. She had very concerned and helpful parents. All of the children were thought of as individuals not just as syndromes.

As we began our first circle time with my guitar handy, Jane looked out the window and said, "Oh no! Here comes Valerie." I soon found why Jane had such angst. Valerie had been in school the year before, but left without explanation. Valerie was a sturdy Native American girl with dark deep set eyes, poor skin, and a mouth that never stopped. Whatever crossed her mind, exited her mouth. She burst through the door shouting, "Hi, Harwood, where is Martha (previous teacher), whose father is he?" (Pointing to me) When Jane told her I was her new teacher, she immediately said, "What's your birthday?" I told her, and she asked, "No, what year too?" I told her then she blurted, "You were born on Thursday." Jane said, "Check it out. I'll bet she is right." She was. Valerie had a gift. Part of her brain worked in mysterious ways, other parts worked minimally. The term "idiot savant" best described Valerie's strange talent. She would remain in my class for three years. In that time she never forgot an acquaintance's birthday but could not remember her phone number. Go figure.

On the drive home after my first day at school, I marveled at the green of the forest, the crystal blue of the sky, and the fast moving Bear River. We had made the right choice. Our small community had a boating lake, tennis courts, a golf course, and a beautiful club house. Things happened slowly in the foothills, it would be a month before we could get phone service. To make a phone call we had a five minute drive to use the pay phone. This was the first new home I ever owned, and I was excited about various projects that new homeowners relish. First priority was a garden. We had plenty of space for it and we planted some fifty species of fruits and vegetables, much to the delight of the local birds and deer. We had so much to learn. Wendy gave up her job but would pursue a real estate license. She soon got into a babysitting co-op which freed time for a job search.

The school day began at 8:45 a.m. when the buses rolled in and ended at 2:30 p.m. Because of the rural nature of the county and the scattering of county school facilities, some of the students spent over two hours a day on the buses. This was a problem in rural areas. Unlike my experience in Oakland, the Pine View parents were very involved with school. With the recent passage of P.L. 94-142, also known as *Education for All Handicapped Children Act,* parents had the right to participate in an educational plan for their child. The law had not been totally implemented in Placer County, but committees were working out the details. In nut shell, the new law guaranteed that all children with special needs receive a free and appropriate public education. Parents were seen as partners in planning their child's individual educational plan (IEP), and the child should be served in the least restrictive environment (LRE). Placer County Office of Ed would spend years dealing with the full implementation of the law. As they say, the devil is in the details.

The first weeks of school went by quietly. Jane was excellent at arts and crafts, putting up bulletin boards, supervising the playground, working in the kitchen, and keeping her teacher in line. I was happy to invite another class to join us at circle time. The children loved to sing even though their singing was usually in the gravel like key of "R." We worked on calendar skills, personal grooming, time, money, and emergency words. Mary was able to read at a second grade level and enjoyed being the belle of the ball. She loved being partnered with other children. The Davids could be gentlemen for the most part, but David A. did have his share of stubborn rants. Although Down children share many of the same physical characteristics, their personalities and cognitive abilities can vary widely.

One day after school, I got a frantic call from Mary's mother. "Did you put Mary on the bus this afternoon?"

I replied, "Of course I did, what is the problem?"

"She didn't get off," she screamed. The Captain (Mary's officious dad) and I are frantic."

It seems that dear Mary had decided to visit downtown Loomis instead of going straight home. Why the bus driver let her get off early was beyond me. Ten minutes later Mary walked through her front door happy as could be. The police had been notified and the "Captain" had been ready to call in the National Guard, and he may have had the power to do so. The next day we presented a lesson on bus safety.

Jane and I attempted to bring the trials and tribulations of the children's outside lives into the classroom. Steven came into the room one morning with a nasty burn across the front of his throat. Jane noticed first and brought Steven to me. "Steve, what happened to your neck?" I asked.

He stuttered that he was riding his bike and he hit a rope. Upon further questioning, Steve confessed that some boys pulled the rope just as he passed them. Apparently he had been the victim of bullying before, but this time the boys went too far. He could have been seriously hurt. "Do you know the boys?"

"Yeah they live near me, they're my friends," he stuttered. I had to reassure good natured Steve that he was not in trouble and that friends don't treat friends that way. I called his mother, and she did not know the circumstances of Steve's "accident" but she suspected that she knew the boys involved. She gave us their names and we contacted the boy's school. The boy's principal was very disturbed. I knew they would be disciplined appropriately. Some sensitivity training needed to be done at their elementary school. I offered to talk to the school staff. We often had to walk the thin line between fear of and naive trust of others. Reluctantly, I had to instruct the children to back away from hugging strangers. It is cute, but preteen children have to know where the lines are drawn. It is a difficult thing to explain, and we spent a lot of time reinforcing a hand shake instead of a hug. The line between fear and trust is foggy. As far as I know Steve had no more neighborhood difficulties and was free to ride his bike in peace.

After three months at Pine View, I felt at home. Jane and I had a good working relationship and we were working together as one. Shortly before Christmas, Wendy and I were invited to my friend Howard's home for a game of cards with friends. Dawn had a cold so we bundled her in a warm blanket and let her rest in a spare bedroom. After a short time, Wendy went to check on our daughter. She rushed into the kitchen and gasped, "We have to get Dawn to the hospital NOW!" Dawn was having a seizure. Her eyes were rolled back, she was rigid and unconscious. We ran to my VW bus and drove as quickly as was safe to the nearest hospital eight long miles away. Howard said he would call the hospital alerting them that an emergency was on the way. The VW doesn't warm up quickly, so we shook from the cold as well as fear while driving north of the speed limit. The emergency room was ready for us and Dawn was rushed to the care of the ER staff. Dawn seemed a bit more alert as the hospital staff examined her. I was very concerned by Dawn's posture, her right hand was clenched and could not relax. The same rigidity I often observed in Cerebral Palsied children. The doctor decided a spinal was in order to rule out meningitis. Things settled down, Dawn was resting, relaxed, and her temperature was on down. The test was negative. We went outside briefly and met with Howard who had followed us to the hospital. Tears ran down our faces as Wendy and I breathed a sigh of relief. We thought of what could have been. Wendy spent the night with Dawn as Howard drove me home. The seizure was caused by a high temperature perhaps we had bundled her too well. The eight mile drive in the cold VW bus helped bring down her temp. I now felt more empathy for parents of special needs children.

That winter my parents visited from New Hampshire. One week would have been fine, but three weeks were a strain on all involved. It was during their visit that I began to run once again. My initial goal was to run the perimeter of Lake of the Pines, a rolling five mile asphalt road. It was painful and slow but after a week I had success. It seems that if I could push beyond two and a half miles I had to finish. This was farther than I had ever run and I felt a wonderful sense of achievement. Part of my weekly routine would be an after school jog three or four days a week. I was able to drop about ten pounds in two months. Running was to be my passion and stress release for twenty-five years.

One morning, Valarie arrived in a particularly foul mood, even for Valerie. Her hair and been attacked by what appeared to have been a weed eater. "What happened to your hair?" Jane shouted.

"My Mom, she cut it all off. She was mad at me," Valerie huffed. "Mom said I couldn't see my Uncle Bobby again." She said as this story took an ominous turn.

"Who is Uncle Bobby?" I joined in.

"He's not really my uncle and Mom said I can't shower with him, no more."

"Valerie did anything else happen?" I asked as we took Val into the hall to continue the questions away from other children.

"Well he wanted to play those games, you know, down there," she said as she pointed between her legs. We let Valerie return to the classroom as I called the County Administration office. They, in turn, contacted the Child Protective Service. That afternoon Valerie was questioned by a detective from their office. Val, though flakey, is not prone to lie. She just doesn't know how. Within a few days we heard that "Uncle Bobby" had been contacted and had a restraining order placed on him. Nothing could be proven, so no charges were ever filed, but we certainly kept our eye out for any disturbing behavior from Valerie.

Teachers have an obligation to report any suspicion of child abuse. In fact, we could be held liable if we did not report questionable acts toward the children under our care. This is always a difficult dilemma—do we accuse a parent or caretaker of suspicious activity whenever we see a bruise, or do we ignore? Luckily, I never had to take a parent to task. In fact, most the parents I dealt with were far beyond reproach.

I was the lowest tenured teacher in the County Office having been the last hired, until just after Christmas. Kathleen was hired to replace a teacher who resigned mid-year. Kathleen and her class joined us for circle time most days and indeed we would team teach and share duties often. One of her students was a Howdy Doody look-alike with a Denis the Menace personality. His name was Chuck, and he often used his angelic looks and good language skills to his devious advantage. Kathleen had a particularly difficult morning with Chuck. She was exasperated and asked if he could be "timed out" in my room. "No problem," I said. This occurred the week before Easter. Jane and the other aides had made cupcakes, and we were to enjoy them immediately after the lunch recess. Chuck remained in my room while the others were on the playground. I had to take a phone call and was out of my room for only a minute. Upon returning, every jelly bean from every cupcake had mysteriously disappeared. Chuck smiled with telltale frosting lingering on his innocent looking face. He blurted out, "I didn't do it" even before I asked about the purloined jelly beans. The entire staff was overcome with laughter over another Chuck incident. He was the bad boy you just had to love. He joined my class the following year but had exhausted his welcome with his foster parents and was moved out of the county to Paradise, California. That was the day we sent Chuck to Paradise.

Another teacher on the staff was Nelly. She was in her forties, overweight, and highly manipulative. I had been warned, by knowing staff members, to keep her at a polite distance. She had befriended our custodian, an all-around good guy named John, and invited him to spend a weekend at her home near Lake Tahoe. John spent that weekend not relaxing in the sun as he intended but instead worked his butt off doing chores for Nelly. Another disturbing trait of hers was to inform parents of the wonderful progress that her fine teaching had achieved. Parents wanted to hear good news, of course, and Nelly gave it to them even though it was far from the truth. This made things very difficult for any teacher who had Nelly's children the following year. I was one of those, "No I'm sorry, but I don't see David reading yet nor doing more than simple math," I had to explain during teacher-parent conferences. I looked like the teacher who could not deliver what the parents so desperately wanted.

The tide turned for Nelly the following year. She came to school one day with a diamond ring and told the entire staff that she was engaged to a lawyer from Reno and would soon be married in a small ceremony. The staff held a wedding shower for her, with cake, gifts, and well wishes. It was a hoax! There was no fiancé, she purchased the ring, and concocted the account. When the administration found out about it, she was dismissed and was given a full severance package in order to avoid a threatened lawsuit. Don't get me started about tenure. News came one day to Pine View that Nelly had shot herself in her lonely Tahoe home. Truly a disturbed soul who should not have been in a teaching position.

On the first Friday of each month, we loaded the children onto buses and headed to a nearby Auburn bowling alley. For some students a ramp and gutter bumpers were provided so they could achieve success, others bowled normally. I enjoyed these junkets for several reasons. We were having a good time with an athletic activity, were reinforcing social skills, and the public would see special needs children acting appropriately. Our scores didn't seem to matter to any of the children, other than David A., who always wanted to win.

In the spring, Special Olympics became a major event in the lives of our children. I included training as part of the curriculum. Most of our kids participated, and the parents were usually enthusiastically cheering them on. I did try to keep my mouth shut with all of the hugging between strangers and our kids, and I succeeded. I had a Special Olympic star in Steven as he blew away any and all competition in all his events.

Placer County Teachers did not belong to a state or a national teacher organization. Instead we formed our own teacher group for negotiations and grievances. Appropriately, it was called PEST, an acronym for Placer Educators and Special Teachers. In my first few years these negotiations worked well and after experiences in Oakland, I was happy we negotiated on a less confrontational level. A good working relationship between administration and staff was the rule in Placer County. We were a small group at the time. As the years wore on, insurance and salary negotiations became more contentious, as was the norm throughout the nation.

In spite of the benefits and salary, like many of my peers, I needed to supplement my salary by working summer school. Teaching pay was adequate in a two salary home, but was a stretch with just one main paycheck. I signed up for the five week summer school with my current class. Not all children were enrolled for the full five weeks and school was dismissed at 1 p.m. We swam two days a week at a local high school pool. Local lifeguards taught swimming, therefore, teaching summer school was not too taxing, especially with Valerie not attending.

One chilly morning at the pool, as we walked to the changing room, my student Bobbie casually pushed a small Down boy named Robbie into the pool. I watched as he slowly sank to the very bottom of the deep end. He just lay there eight feet below with a look of bewilderment on his face. My first thought was, "Gee, that water looks cold." I put that aside, kicked off my shoes, and dove straight down pulling Robbie to the surface. He came up laughing as if to say, "Let's do that again, and why are you all wet?"

After summer school, Wendy and I packed Dawn and the VW bus, heading for wilds of British Columbia for a two week camping trip. It ended too soon and I was back at school before Labor Day.

Special Ed. teachers were now subject to the rigors of implementing the new Public Law 94-142 in earnest. We would have to have individual educational plans for each child and implement them throughout the school year. These IEP plans were put together by a team of the classroom teacher, administrator, parents, and any additional involved professional. At this point it was usually myself and a parent. Our administrator generally just signed off on the plan. This was to change drastically in years to come when IEP meetings often took hours and had a huge cast of characters.

The new school year began with little fanfare. It seemed no more than a continuation of summer school minus the swimming. We welcomed two new students. Kelly, a lovely, tall ten-year-old girl with long strawberry blonde hair, but a vacant stare. She had few verbal skills but was always compliant and sweet. Then there was Tim. He, too, had little communication ability, but was far from compliant. He often curled into a tight knot, twisted his hands overhead, looked me in the eye while declared, "Mad you, T"—meaning "I'm mad at you Tebow." Jane was not outside of Tim's angst. He would threaten her announcing, "Dad get you, Harwood." I found my solace with Kelly's few verbalizations. With a prompt from Jane, Kelly would say, "Tebow is a wonderful man." Thank you, Kelly, you often made my day.

Before Christmas that year, I was devastated with the news that Jane had lung cancer. She was in her early forties, had never smoked, was not overweight, and ate a very healthy diet. She was a single mother of two adult children. Sometimes life seems so unfair. Jane vowed she would get through this crisis and would work as often and as long as possible. I promised to help as much as I could. She persevered and missed very few days that year. I admired her endurance and courage.

My class went smoothly for the most part my second year. Valerie, the Davids, Steven, Heather, and the rest knew the routine and made life easy for Jane and me. We had our usual tantrums, crisis', breakthroughs, and disappointments. I had the guidance of my friend, Howard, as a speech therapist. He advised us to use a new approach to language. His suggestion was called total language. We would use sign language and verbalizations at the same time giving visual as well as verbal clues to speech. At this point I became "Tebow" with both hands making the "T" (thumbs between first and second fingers in a fist) sign and tying a bow in the air. The kids caught on quickly and seemed to prosper with this new method. Not all parents bought into the method, however, believing that their children signing maybe be interpreted as a sign of deafness.

After Christmas, I was introduced to a new student. Parry had very special needs. He was my oldest student and my most impaired. He was legally blind and the little hearing he possessed was non-functional. I would have the assistance of the visually impaired and the deaf/hard of hearing specialists but only on a consulting basis. He was fixated on his self-stimulating hand movements. I had to get right in Parry's face to give any instructions or he would ignore me. His mom was an overwrought single parent who loved her child but was in serious need of relief. She moved to Placer County in order to give Parry a better education. The pressure was on. Parry would have nothing to do with the other children and they, in turn, gave Parry a wide berth. He was unaware of his deviant behavior, thus it was difficult to take him out of school on trips. His hands were often in his crotch, he would often strike out at other children, and he had many loud nonsensical vocalizations. In short, he needed to be socialized first and foremost.

I was able to attend a three-day conference on the Education of the Blind-Deaf at the University of Arizona. I found that I wasn't alone with my frustrations. New strategies and techniques were introduced. I was able to borrow books and materials from the Blind-Deaf Education Association. More importantly, I understood Parry's frustrations and difficulties. I was determined to push the administration for a special aide for Parry. Neither Jane nor I was able to delegate enough time to meet Parry's educational needs.

A short walk from Pine View, a new school, as yet unnamed, was being built. It would house the PCOE moderately impaired classes with students from nine years through twenty-one years of age. It would be a state of the art facility with a modern gym, workshop, art room, full kitchen, and a vocational program. Our Special Ed. supervisor would have his office in the building. Unfortunately teachers had little input into the design of the structure or landscape. The site would have a small lake and with fancy grassy landscaping, but no playground. The children would not be allowed near the grass or lake. It was for show only. I would be one of the six teachers to occupy the new school. Faculty meetings in 1978/79 year included all six teachers who would be working in the new school. We had to bargain for assignments. Kathleen was chosen to begin the new vocational program. She would work in the kitchen but also with the Regional Occupational Program. Dale, a former college football player and strict disciplinarian, would be in the shop room. He and Jim, who had the most seniority, would work with the oldest and most advanced students. Mrs. Parry had the arts and crafts room. Mrs. Roskelly and I had standard classrooms with the younger children. I reluctantly agreed to work with the children with the most verbal and developmental needs. I looked upon the assignment as a challenge as I did with my autistic class. I often walked my class down the wooded path to watch the construction of *their* new school.

This was the first year that I was aware of the impact that computers could have in the classroom. A teacher in the physically disabled program became our tech specialist. We had access to three Apple computers. In 1978 we were impressed that we could actually write reports without a typewriter. Wow! It was years before I had my own computer in school. Technology has vast implications in classrooms for the disabled populations. The future was just around the corner.

After school, I took up running more often to relieve stress. I began competing in local and regional races. The payoff was losing weight, becoming physically stronger, and igniting my competitive juices that had long been in hibernation. Another summer school program came and went. Jane took the summer off as she tried to recover from chemotherapy, and I taught that summer with a new aide.

CHAPTER 11

SECRET RAVINE SCHOOL

Our new school was named after its, physical location. It was just downhill from the other two county schools, in a hollow named Secret Ravine. Secret Ravine was a single-story building of butterscotch colored brick with lots of windows. My classroom was the first encountered while entering the building. We had lovely views of the foothills, a small lake, and the Union Pacific railroad tracks.

The plan was to provide the children with a team teaching approach. In reality the plan was flawed, because each teacher wanted full control of their own classes. The three youngest classes were often together in my room, for guitar time, singing, and rhythm activities ala Buzz Glass. Mrs. Perry took my class for arts and crafts lesson, while Mrs. Roskelly brought children to her room for more advanced reading and math activities. Few of my children were reading or doing more than basic counting. I was asked to be the Physical Ed. teacher for the three youngest classes. Too often, however, cooperation was lacking, and I was as guilty as anyone.

I had the usual cast of characters, the Davids, Tim, Heather, Parry, Kelly, et all. Missing from my class, but not the school, were Valarie and Mary; both had moved on to a new class. I had two new students.

Kirk, a handsome boy with minimal Cerebral Palsy, had good language skills, was well behaved, and had a likable smile. He had been in classes for the physically disabled and was a favorite of Heather's. His dad was a deputy sheriff and mom a very involved parent.

Trish was an impish-like wonder. This girl was petite, with deep set eyes, was very verbal, but had to be encouraged to participate. She was able to read surprising well. She would become the star performer during school performances as the master of ceremonies. She had no fear of performing in front of a crowd, once she began. Her other surprising skill; she was a gifted piano player. She could listen to a musical piece, go immediately to the piano and repeat the song note for note. I'm certain that Trish today would be in regular class with help from a resource teacher and be diagnosed as Asperger's. She did lack social skills, difficulty with relationships, and would tune out adults unless forced to respond.

One fall morning I was visited by Kirk's mother. She asked if she could observe the class in progress. "Of course," I said, although I was uncomfortable being observed for an entire day. I knew that I was being evaluated, but I didn't know why. She sat quietly throughout the morning, went with the children to lunch, and then to the playground. After lunch, we had PE. That day we joined another class in the gym for hockey. We used soft pucks and plastic sticks. Hockey at Secret Ravine was controlled mayhem. I tried to keep the sticks on the ground, but slapped shins were inevitable. Kirk's mother burst out in fits of laughter. She had hardly spoken to me during the entire day. Finally she came up to me smiling. "Mr. Thibeault, please tell me that you played hockey yesterday," she inquired. "Yeah, we played all week at PE. Why?" I answered.

"Kirk came home last night and told his father and me that you let the children hit him with sticks. I had to see what was going on. I'm so glad to see Kirk participating at PE and think your class is wonderful for our son." After a day feeling like a fish on a hook, I was thrilled to be released.

Heather posed another problem. She wore a helmet and walked with the aid of crutches, but her balance was still not controlled. As much as we tried to protect her, falls were inevitable. When she did fall, she literally took it on the chin. She could not protect herself because her arms were attached to sleeves on the crutches. Seeing her fall was like watching a lumberjack felling a tree. Poor Heather's chin was a mosaic of scares. Her parents had been understanding, not wanting Heather to be overprotected. We did try to work on Heather's mobility and balance. I attempted to teacher her to sit when she felt she was losing her balance. Her bottom was softer than her chin.

Our Program supervisor, Jack, worked for the County Office of Education as a psychologist but true to form had no teaching experience. He was not involved with the curriculum but was more of a building manager and official paper signer. In fairness to Jack, he had other programs to supervise as well as Secret Ravine. He once wrote a newsletter to the parents stating, "We are attempting to work the bugs out of our hot lunch program." Luckily his keen secretary covered for him and changed the wording. Jack was ready to retire. We all felt that it wouldn't come soon enough. Most of his conversations with the staff seemed to be about fishing. Unfortunately, two years later Jack's wife developed cancer and succumbed just before his retirement. Jack's smoking caught up with him and lung cancer claimed him a few months later. So much for a happy retirement.

I struggled with a learning development conundrum. I realized that my kids had to be able to establish how things differed in order to learn. Was this the lowest common denominator? I had students sorting, big from little, green from blue, round from square, etc... For those children more knowledgeable, I would have them show me the differences between, many and few, light and dark, fast and slow. Lessons could progress from that point into more subtle differences. This approach gave me direction and allowed the kids a measure of success no matter what level they were working on.

Personal hygiene was also stressed at Secret Ravine. We had shower rooms for boys and girls, lockers for gym clothes, dental hygiene lessons, and laundry machines for clothes and towels. We also had a nutritionist, Kathy, working part time on a grant. She was kept very busy giving lessons on weight control and diet. She assisted in the kitchen, in the classroom, and assisted parents with nutritional planning.

One of her projects was to screen for high cholesterol. After receiving parental permissions, a blood test was given by our school nurse. It involved a small blood draw from a prick on the finger. We were the first class to be tested. I sent the Davids in first with no problems. Both emerged from the nurse's office with a happy face sticker. Next was Heather.

She screamed like death was at her door. She returned to our room and announced, "They are cutting us." All hell broke loose. "Not me," screamed Kirk. Even shy Trish verbalized her reluctance. "I don't want to go," she cried. Our poor nurse gave up at that point as I could not drag another youngster into her lair. I think the older classes fared better. We did have number of children in the school with diabetes and were used to blood pricks on daily basis.

Parry continued to be my biggest challenge. The visual handicapped specialist and the itinerate deaf/hard of hearing specialist visited occasionally, but were overworked and stretched thin. Jane and I knew basic sign language and this is how we communicated with Parry after getting in his face because of his limited vision. One of the most used signed phrases for Parry was, "No penis play in school, you play with penis at home." This did not discourage him much and his crotch grabbing was a constant problem. Parry had spent many months in hospitals as a baby and a toddler. He had a particular fondness for men dressed in suits, because his doctors were the only men in his background whom he saw routinely. He would sometimes jump a man from behind and straddle him, maybe appropriate behavior for a two-year-old happy to see his doctor, but not for a twelve-year-old and a school visitor. We had US Congressman Bizz Johnson visit the school for a dedication of a new flag. Just then, who should I see but Parry leaving his seat and making a beeline toward our distinguished visitor. I reached him just before the attack. Somehow I wished I had missed. I was still promised an additional aide for Parry, maybe a congressional embarrassment would have hastened the process.

Discipline was seldom a serious problem in my class, the exception (there is always an exception), was Tim. He continued his stubbornness and unwillingness to follow simple instructions. One day he was particularly vexed. He refused to eat his lunch, stay in his seat, or participate in any class work. One of the lunch recess supervisors interrupted my meal saying, "Tim just bolted from the playground." We were prepared for runaways. Dale jumped into his vehicle heading toward the main road which was a busy thoroughfare. I ran up the trail toward Pine View School where I spotted Tim hiding under a tree. He knew he was in serious trouble but refused to follow me back to school. I had to stand behind him pushing as he marched reluctantly toward the building, Tim ready to run again and me wondering what to do next. He just kept saying, "Mad you, Tebow, mad you." He still had the devil in his eye. I sat him on one of our new couches in the hall next to my class. As I watched, he twisted and smiled at me as a dark stain spread on the cushion beneath him. He not only peed, but soiled himself deliberately. I was slightly south of furious. I dragged him into the shower after forcing him to wipe the soiled cushion, made him strip, turned on the shower, and drove him into the spray. He yelled, "Cold."

I yelled back, "Then clean yourself quickly."

He was shaking from the cold as well as the anger until the stream turned warm. Punishment fitting the crime? I'm not sure. I know, I would never have given a cold shower in these politically correct days, but this was 1979. I gave him a warm towel, clean clothes, and waited for him outside the shower room. I called his parents leaving a message about our incident. They never responded, and Tim never forgot his shower.

Kathleen had a much more threatening incident. A new nineteen-year-old student was enrolled in her vocational classroom. Kathleen weighed one hundred five pounds dripping wet. Her new boy was six feet and easily weighted two-twenty. During his first week at Secret Ravine, he blew. I'm not sure what participated the clash, but he was totally out of control. Kathleen ran to me for help. I saw that things were beyond our abilities and we needed more help. I said, "Call Dale and Jim." We never thought of Jack. The new boy was in the gym, and he had a baseball bat in his hands, threatening to hit whoever came near. Four of us surrounded him and tried to talk him down while not provoking him further. After what seemed a week, the bat was released and the episode was over. Jack was called after the fact. The boy was expelled from school because he was a danger to the faculty, other students, and himself. I felt that we had let him down.

Safety is always a concern with our children and yet we had to get them out of school and into the community as often as possible. We had access to a county station wagon for field trips. The small town of Loomis had a perfect little downtown to demonstrate safety skills. We would use the crosswalk practicing walking with the traffic light, keeping to the right side of a sidewalk, or being quiet in the library. One morning while walking down the Loomis main street, sweet Kelly must have been fixated on birds, clouds, or the wind. She turned and walked directly into the line of traffic. I was able to grab her just before an impact with a distracted driver's vehicle. She smiled at me as if nothing had occurred and said, "Tebow is a wonderful man." Thanks Kelly.

As the year worn on with little drama, Jane's health was not good and many days I had a substitute aide. Jane was very courageous, however, and worked often when she should have stayed home. I suffered from migraine headaches in the spring of that year, which paled against Jane's health problems. I never did find out why I had them or how to avoid the trauma. I continued to run after school and felt it a great stress reliever and it seemed to help with the headaches.

It's been said that moving, changing jobs, and having a small child, are heavy stress inducing events in one's life. Both Wendy and I were feeling the increasing tension. My Yankee reticence to explore feelings only added to our increasing anxiety. My solution was to pound more pavement. That wasn't working. I managed to run two marathons that year which gave me a sense of accomplishment that the job lacked. Dawn continued to be a bright spark in those days. Her large eyes, bright smile, and precocious personality never failed to bring a smile to all she came in contact with.

Toward the end of the year a faculty meeting was held in order to plan for next year's assignments. No one other than myself was anxious to change positions. I found teaching the same group of children for three straight years less than challenging. I let everyone know that I was feeling stale and would like a change. Reluctantly, I agreed to work another year with the same children. In order to placate me, I was given a new assignment for the summer program. I worked at the Newcastle School for the Physically Handicapped. The five-week program was both stimulating and rewarding. I had the advantage of working with an experienced aide, Ruby. She was a personal friend and a pleasure to be around. It was also refreshing to work with new staff members. The small class consisted of the oldest children in the school. I had five boys and one girl. Most had Cerebral Palsy with varying degrees of involvement. One boy had Muscular Dystrophy and was in a motorized chair. Toileting and feeding were physically demanding tasks for the staff. I learned how to safely transfer students from wheelchairs, to standing tables, to mats on the floor. We had on-campus physical therapists, a speech therapist, and a psychologist as support staff. Luckily Ruby was familiar with two of the CP boy's speech patterns. I had to learn listening patiently and not attempt to finish their sentences. One boy, Jeff, tried very hard to be understood. He was bright and became frustrated when his attempts at speech fell on my untrained ears. Jeff had a word-board but floundered trying to point and had a limited word list to choose from. I hope wherever he is now, he has full use of all the technology available to him.

That summer was my first experience, but not last, with Muscular Dystrophy. It is a devastating disease that takes the young. Most victims are boys and at that time they seldom lived beyond their teens. Eddie, the MD boy in my class, was rightfully angry at his fate. Three years before, he was a happy healthy fourth grader when without warning he began the downward trend that is MD. Emotionally I could deal with children who have been impaired since birth. It was easy for me to accept them and their disabilities, but watching a child without hope and in continual decline was difficult.

I foolishly volunteered to pace a runner in the Western States One Hundred Mile Run which climbs from Squaw Valley and travels one hundred miles on rocky trails to Auburn. During the race, I asked a runner named Bill if he needed help from a pacer for the final twenty-five miles. I asked Bill, "What is your marathon personal best?"

He said, "About a three hours and twenty minutes."

No problem, I thought, I ran a three-fifteen and he had already run seventy-five miles. I should be able to keep up. While heading up a two mile hill I was running trying to stay with Bill as he was walking comfortably. I remarked on his exceptional walking skill. He said, "Walking is my sport." Stupidly, I asked if he competed as a race walker.

"Well," said Bill, "I was in the Munich Olympics and held the American fifty kilometer record."

"Oh." I humbly kept my mouth shut and just kept running. Bill finished third out of two hundred plus starters. I was enamored with the race and was involved with it for the next thirty years in one form or another.

After summer school we a had house exchange in Flagstaff, Arizona, a visit to the Grand Canyon and a few weeks respite, before I faced another year at Secret Ravine with the lowest functioning class. I had the same great group of kids and none of the faculty had changed.

During the summer, an athletic field was built behind the school. I measured a four hundred meter track so we could train for Special Olympics as well as participate in other sports. Dale and Jim had organized a flag football team that would compete against another special school. I was able to include a few of my students in the games. I'm not sure if we won or lost. It didn't matter. Our kids were happy to participate. One of our students, Lenny, was asked by me to pull the flag off a rival during a play. He looked down pulled both his own flags and returned them to me with a self-satisfied smile.

My student, Steve, had such a gift for running. He had grown tall and lean. I would lead him while running around the track asking him to follow me closely. His attitude was tremendous and his times improved rapidly. One day I went to a junior high track meet and timed the four hundred meter run. In this dual school meet Steve's time would have put him in second place. Unfortunately he was never given the opportunity to compete against his more normal peers. He just loved to run.

Jane was not doing well in her battle against cancer. She looked ashen, had lost weight, and twice had emergency procedures to drain fluid from her lungs. Surgery was not an option and time was running out for her. She continued to stress that she wanted to be in the classroom as much as she was able. She needed to feel useful. I was finally assigned another aide to help supervise Parry and his multiple needs, but also as a break for Jane. Her name was Cindy. She was only twenty, had long blonde hair, was fit, but also inexperienced. She had a basic understanding of sign language. I assigned her mostly to work with Parry, and to relieve Jane whenever possible. I took a lot of ribbing from Dale and Jim for having such a young looker in my room. Cindy, in truth, had a troubled past having bounced around several foster homes, and her home life was on the skids. This left a certain tough edge to her demeanor and her language was sometimes rough. She and Jane sometimes bumped heads, but I tried to sooth any problems before they arose. She was good with Parry and he seemed to be taken with her. As the year wore on Jane missed more and more time, and Cindy became indispensable in the class.

Our team teaching experiment was not working out well once again, but I was willing to work as the Physical Education Specialist for the younger classes. I often used the activities, rhythms, and dances, taught to me by Buzz Glass and Jack Capon as inspiration. I did some task analysis with standard games. When playing hockey, I positioned teams inside colored hula hoops, red hoops or blue depending on one's team. Players had to stay in their hoops, thus eliminating many bruised shins and keeping players in correct positions. I modified basketball as well. I used our ball cages as baskets and again limited the space in which players could travel. After three dribbles one had to pass or shoot. I would sometimes demand three passes before anyone took a shot. If playing with less skilled students I would use Nerf balls. We played volleyball with beach balls or balloons. I really enjoyed adapting the rules to make games more successful but still challenging for all. Both Cindy and I participated in the games acting as role models and at the same time attempting to keep order.

The other plus with teaching the PE classes was the daily lessons in hygiene and dressing skills. Everyone had to change into gym clothes and shower after the sessions. Cindy handled the girls locker rooms while I the boys. While I had PE classes going on, Mrs. Perry often had arts and crafts in her room. Mrs. Roskelly took some of my higher performing students for additional reading or math lessons. Kathleen, Dale, and Jim handled the older students and did their own thing.

Lunch was also a learning experience. Most of the older students worked in the kitchen, had lunch prep, or clean up duties. At times we did some planting and harvesting in a garden behind the building. Our nutritionist, when she wasn't asking for blood, gave lessons on diet and food prep. Our school nurse gave lessons in dental brushing, hand washing, and feminine hygiene for the older girls.

That fall I accepted a job teaching for Chapman College. Chapman maintains a college program on many armed service bases throughout the country as well as a campus in Orange, California. I taught a four hour class once a week. It was held at Marysville High School, near Beal Air Force Base. The class was state mandated entitled, "Special Education in the Elementary School." It was a requirement for all applicants of an elementary teaching credential. Each Tuesday that fall, I drove the fifty miles on hilly roads just after dismissal at Secret Ravine. I was paid according to enrollment and had fewer than ten students. The salary was not why I took this job. I enjoyed the intellectual challenge of progressing from teaching my moderately impaired students to a graduate level class in an hour's time span. There was a required text that was not of much value. I prepared a lecture of an hour or more each week but most time was spent in class discussions. I gave the students sensitivity training as well as some insights into the behaviors of the special needs students they were likely to encounter in their classes. Of course, we had to discuss the legal aspects of PL 94-142. Most of my students were currently teaching or substitute teaching on partial credentials. Not only did I have to grade the Chapman students, but they had to grade me. I did get excellent reviews and enjoyed the discussions, but the travel after school was wearing. I would not get home until after ten at night and spent a good deal of time preparing the lectures the night before each class. I worked only one semester for Chapman. I'd often thought of teaching on the college level and now knew I could handle the job, should an offer ever arise.

That fall, I was able to pass the state exam for the administrative credential. I applied, and was granted the credential, not knowing if I would ever use it. It seems a shame that once a teacher reaches a certain level on the salary scale he or she can't advance salary wise unless there are increases to the salary schedule. Administration is the only path to a higher pay. Even Jamie Escalante, the teacher portrayed in the film "Stand and Deliver," had to take a salary cut to transfer for LA to Sacramento Schools. Can you imagine a businessman of such high regard taking a cut in pay to move into a new firm?

Later that year, I was called into the Office of the Superintendent of Special Services. Bruce Becker, the associate superintendent, talked about Jack's failing health and asked me to take over for him on a part-time basis. I would also continue teaching part-time. I knew that this would mean working more hours for very little extra pay, however, it could lead to a full time administrative position. I thought long and hard about this offer, then turned it down. What I liked most about my present position was working with the children. My least favorite thing was attending endless meetings. Administration equals endless meetings and conflicts. It just wasn't me. After I turned down the job, our current school psychologist took over for the ailing Jack.

Kathleen had another new student. His name was Billy and he was a six-foot-two, two hundred thirty pound black eighteen-year-old. He was a foster child and a gentle soul with a penchant for wandering. Billy was verbal but would become silent when pressed to talk. After only two weeks in school, Kathleen received a call from the Roseville police asking if she knew a William B. He had been found roving around a Roseville neighborhood at one in the morning. He refused to answer questions but did say he knew a Kathleen at Secret Ravine School. Roseville is a mostly white Sacramento suburb. Billy's nighttime adventure and silence didn't go over well with the local cops. Apparently some neighbor saw him on the street, called the police, and Billy resisted. The poor big lug was handcuffed and hauled into the drunk tank. Like many foster parents, Billy's could not abide his antisocial behavior. He left Secret Ravine, and we never heard from him again.

We had several wonderful foster homes in the county. One, the Mitchells, consisted of six older high functioning girls, two of whom they eventually adopted. Their care was second to none. Another family, the Dustons, provided great foster care to three or four of our children, my Kelly included. For some reason, there was a suggestion of sexual abuse by Mr. Duston. How this occurred, I never found out. Child Protective Services arrived at school prepared with anatomically complete dolls and questions for all of the Duston foster children in closed rooms. One very together student told the officers, "My dad never showed his dick to nobody. He wouldn't do that." Ultimately no charges were filed as there was not a shred of evidence of wrong doing. However, the damage was done and the Dustons left the foster care business. Luckily most of their children were placed in the county and stayed at Secret Ravine. This was another example of someone's good intentions leading to bad results.

One of PL 94-142's requirements was in direct conflict with the aims of Secret Ravine. The Least Restrictive Environment (LRE) clause was intended to keep special needs students with their more normal peers as much as possible. Parents were within their rights to demand placement in the LRE. Segregating students in a special school was in direct conflict with the LRE provision. The writing was on the wall. Local districts were going to take back many of their students and Secret Ravine would change for good. There were both positives and negatives to this. Secret Ravine had wonderful facilities that met the needs of our students that local schools could not duplicate. However, they were not being integrated with their normal peers as the law dictates.

Because of the LRE clause, new positions were to be created in the County Office of Education. More special education students in regular classes meant that more ancillary staff would be need to offer services in district schools. One of those was Adapted Physical Education (APE). I wasn't sure what the requirements for the APE position were, but I was intrigued. I made an appointment with our Director of Special Education to find out what it was all about. Bruce Becker was not really sure what the position would entail. He stated that the State Department of Ed hadn't delivered all of the particulars to the districts. He did say that I could apply for the position, if I had the okay from the State Director of Physical Education, Jeannie Bartell. I made an appointment with her.

Jeannie had her office in the huge intimidating California State Department of Education Building. Jeannie, however, was very welcoming. She, too, was struggling with how to handle the new regulations for the Adapted PE Program. She stated that she saw the programs as a blend of PE and Special Ed. I explained that I had been teaching the PE at Secret Ravine. Jeannie said that she had no problem grandfathering me into the program, in fact, she welcomed staff with Special Ed. backgrounds. She gave me a letter for Bruce stating that she had no objections to my becoming the PCOE APE (excuse all the letters). He in turn offered me the position for the 1981-1982 school year. He told me that he would work out how the position would be run, and I told him that I would attend Sacramento State University and take the proper course work to get a full credential, if it became necessary. I was more comfortable finishing out the current school year with my kids knowing that it would be my last.

In the spring Jane became more impaired with her illness and had to leave work. She said she hoped to return, but never did. Cindy took over full-time and Parry was again a shared responsibility.

Wendy was going to school at night and working in a Real Estate Office during the day. Our marriage was under pressure and my lack of sharing feelings wore on Wendy. Her insistence that I open up drove me even deeper into silence. I felt that if I did more around the house, I would get a pass. I began a project to build a solar greenhouse attached to our home. It wasn't the answer. The more distant I felt from Wendy, the more distance I physically ran. Running away from problems, I guess. I raced often on the weekends anything from five kilometers to marathons and it was my passion as well as my escape.

I was anxious about the new position and read what little I could find on Adapted PE. No one in the County Office could offer any help other than wait until the fall and there should be more direction from the State. I did further embrace my role as the PE instructor at Secret Ravine. I improvised even more games and activities with Adapted PE in mind. We did light warm ups, skills, then followed up with a game of some kind. Cindy was very athletic and we both participated in the games. This was a role that Jane was unable to play even when she was well. I was able to get a run in during lunch recess and as a result was already dressed for PE. After PE, I supervised the boys showering and dressing before heading back to the classroom where the last hour was spent reviewing the day's work or in quiet time.

Late in the spring, word came that Jane was in hospice care. I visited her at her home, told her how much she meant to me, and how much I admired her courage. Her son was there and I told him to please keep in touch even if Jane was unable to do so. He was not very good at communicating, but said he would try. The other aides at school also visited with her often. The children were all aware that their "Harwood" was sick and we let them know that she still cared for them. I personally was emotionally broken by Jane's condition. I had not lost a close friend since a classmate died in Junior High. I talked to Cindy frequently about how shattered I felt.

During the last month of school, Cindy arrived with a black eye and bruises on her arms. She was reluctant to talk about it, but I insisted. Her boyfriend, once a local football hero, was now a working stiff who partied too much. They had an argument during which he grabbed and slapped her. I knew he could be psychologically abusive, but never saw evidence of physical abuse until then. She was afraid to return to her apartment and asked me to accompany her home so she could pack clothes and move into a friend's spare room. I felt very protective of her and said of course I would. After that incident we talked about relationships frequently. She needed help, I needed acceptance.

The last week of school I got a call from Jane's son saying that she had died that night. I was blown away. I had a marathon scheduled on that Saturday in nearby Davis. Cindy asked if she could get a ride with me to visit a friend at the University. Well, it's an old and familiar story. There was no friend. I let things get the better of me against my better judgment. I ran the race grieving for Jane and smarting from guilt. The ninety degree temperatures and twenty six miles hurt, but not as much as the pain of remorse. The ride back to Auburn was mostly silent. I told Cindy I had made a mistake and it would not happen again. She understood and seemed to agree.

I had two weeks off before summer school began, when I would once more work with physically disabled students in the PH School. My Catholic upbringing reared its' head. I told Wendy that I did not go to Davis alone and had been unfaithful. She was rightfully fuming, hurt, and bitter. Could we repair the damage? Bottom line, we could not. The injury had been done, the cuts were too deep. I sought solace in Cindy. My heart broke for Dawn, and I tried to let her know the separation had nothing to do with her. I rented a two-room apartment in Auburn and made a promise that Dawn would always have her own room in my home. Cindy spent many nights with me, but not when I had Dawn. Wendy and I arranged a separation agreement. Tuesdays would be Dawn and Dad night, and I would have her on alternate weekends. Wendy would keep the Lake of the Pines house and I would eventually move into a rental house we had in Auburn. Dawn and I traveled to New Hampshire after summer school to break the news to my family.

Cancer dug its angry talons deep into our staff that year. In twelve months' time five members of our Secret Ravine/Pine View "family" were struck with the disease. Jack and his wife, a school janitor, Jane, and late in the summer, Wendy. All, but Wendy, died that year. Wendy's breast cancer added to my sense of guilt and failure. I let her know that we would remain married, though separated, so she could maintain her much needed health insurance. I also said that I would take Dawn as much and as often as she felt necessary. Luckily and courageously, Wendy survived her bout with the demon and is doing fine to this day.

The summer certainly was spent in transition. I settled into the new apartment, traded in the old VW wagon for a small Ford truck, and ran my first ultramarathon, a distance beyond the twenty-six point two marathon miles. I joined a group of runners who were interested in the Western States trail that stretched from Squaw Valley to my home town of Auburn. We covered the first seventy-eight miles of the trail in three days. This event, the High Sierra Three Step, was really a running party of, camping, singing, and feasting in the evenings while running the trail in the day. The Three Step became an annual end of summer event that lasted for ten years. Through this annual party, I developed a new circle of friends and a new way of thinking about life. My choice of Adapted PE fit this new approach like a glove. Now it was time to get down to business.

Gene Thibeault

CHAPTER 12

ADAPTED PE THE EARLY YEARS

"Adapted Physical Education (APE) is the art and science of developing, implementing, and monitoring a carefully designed physical education instructional program for a learner with a disability, based on a comprehensive assessment, to give the learner the skills necessary for a lifetime of rich leisure, recreation, and sport experiences to enhance physical fitness and wellness."

I was presented this description by Bruce Becker when I showed up for work the first day of my new career. The real guidelines were yet to be in place. Bruce gave me two weeks to put together a program. I would be the only one doing the job in the entire county, and he expected me to work primarily with children having the greatest need in regular classes. He also suggested that I spend part of my time with the PCOE special classes that were housed in regular schools. He wanted me to eventually work with a caseload of about thirty students. Because I worked for the County Office of Education, my duties could be in as many as eleven districts and fifty schools. Each school had its own agenda, schedule, and administrators. How to begin? It seemed overwhelming. Placer County is mostly rural and stretches from the Sacramento Valley towns of Roseville and Lincoln to the Sierra communities of Truckee and Lake Tahoe, a distance of over ninety miles. I would have to use my car and would be reimbursed for mileage. There would be a lot of "windshield time." Bruce would be my immediate supervisor, and I would report to him directly. I was given a desk in a small office at the School for the Physically Handicapped and shared that space with three school nurses. They were a good source of information and very professional. My first task was to develop a cover letter and referral form to be used by the Special Ed. directors in each district. Bruce had already written a letter of introduction. Some districts had only one school, but others had as many as seven or eight. I chose not to work in the high schools initially, if at all possible. They had physical education teachers who should be equipped to meet the needs of their special children. Unfortunately, I found this was seldom the case. Too often a disabled student sat in the library or just kept score during Physical Education. The county special class teachers should provide physical education to their own students as part of their general curriculum. I would try to give them some demonstrations and guidelines when there was time. These County classes are where I began my first weeks as an "APE." Setting up meetings with the district Special Education directors and or the principals was only the beginning of developing a caseload. PCOE had specialist for the blind and visually handicapped, deaf and hard of hearing, and other low incidence categories. Low incidence children were those whose disabilities were seldom found in the general school population. Individual districts relied on the County Office to provide services for these students while housing them in their own schools. APE was another low incidence program. I met with these special itinerate teachers. They welcomed the services I could provide as their students seldom received appropriate physical education. Other administrators and Special Ed. directors were skeptical and thought my services were another County incursion into their territory. I had to sell a program as well as develop it. Face to face meetings with staffs throughout the county was my approach. I requested a mailbox in each school and met with the all-important school secretaries that I would have to pass to enter each school; sometimes a daunting task. I quickly ordered equipment such as hula hoops, balls, jump ropes, bean bags, and the like. Equipment had to be lightweight, portable, durable, and hopefully have multiple uses. I met with school principals and requested a space to hold my classes. Working on playgrounds, in hallways, spare rooms, cafeterias, but seldom in gyms or multipurpose rooms would be the norm. I found the school custodians very helpful and I courted them. I met with the few physical education teachers in my assigned schools. There were almost none in the elementary schools, but the middle schools usually had both male and female teachers who instructed hundreds of children each week. They were suspicious of a new program, and didn't welcome advice from a County Specialist, especially one with no experience.

The county office already had a small staff of occupational therapists. I counseled with them about caseloads, driving times, which administrators were helpful, which were didn't care, and which were downright hostile to outsiders. I received word from Bruce that my services were requested in the Tahoe-Truckee district on a weekly basis. This meant a drive up Interstate 80, an hour trip and visiting five schools, a big chunk out of the week. I had no office computer, nor cell phone, only a pager. I would write my reports in longhand and have them typed by loyal Sam (Samantha), the PH School secretary. Sam was a small women with the gravel voice of a chronic smoker. She had an inoffensive approach when questioning me about a report. It always began with "Gene, here's what." That was usually the preamble to my redoing a narrative. I would arrive at my desk on Monday mornings with a stack of written reports ready to be typed and filed by Sam. My penmanship and spelling have always been atrocious, but Sam would have corrected reports ready for my review the following Monday. I did most of my paperwork at my home office. Sam's boss was Lila who was a jovial school nurse supervisor who would soon be my boss. Adapted PE was strange to her, but we learned the ins and outs together. Lila and I worked together for over eighteen years. A relationship sometimes strained, but we were always able to work things out.

My best work was always done in the AM. Throughout my APE career, I would write and later type reports at six in the morning with my coffee. I was often chided for leaving schools early, but felt justified because of my early morning starts. When IEP meetings became much more of a group pow-wow this too would change. It was often past five PM when meetings broke up. I was, at first, expected to attend IEPs for each child in my caseload. This proved difficult and often impossible. Some schools, such as Foresthill, held their IEPs on Tuesday mornings before school. Foresthill was a forty minute drive from Auburn on a narrow hilly road. Not going to happen. I developed a routine of presenting a report along with a page of goals and objectives to the Special Education coordinator the week before an IEP. Parents could call me with questions or concerns after the meeting. I did attend many meetings early in the APE program and met with most parents. I found in the first few months that I could meet with just parents and an administrator while writing my part of an existing IEP as an addendum. It seemed the rules were constantly changing and becoming more complicated as the years wore on.

I was challenged with hours of driving time. I often ate, managed files (not while driving), and planned activities while in the car. I would work the valley schools on one day, the Auburn area schools on another, up to Tahoe midweek, the more outlying schools another day, save one morning for the testing of new students, and attending a few school meetings in the afternoon. I sometimes put over a thousand miles on my expense reports. My mileage started from the County Offices in Auburn, unless I was headed east to Tahoe, then I could track miles as soon as I hit the freeway. Setting up a schedule is always traumatic. I had to see children when I was at their school. This led to conflicts with reading, math, assemblies, field trips, along with other numerous disruptions. Classroom teachers were usually, but not always obliging. If push came to shove, the parents were the final arbitrators even more so than the school principals. If I had only one child in a school, I needed to know if he was absent. I asked the schools to notify Sam who would then attempt to reach me. The pager I was given seldom worked. In short if a child was a no go, I sat in the car or went and got coffee until the next appointment. I became intimately acquainted with coffee shops throughout the county. I knew where all the good muffins could be found, hopefully with free newspapers, and a friendly staff.

So I was set. I had a county road map. I had met directors, principals, school secretaries, and janitors. I had a car loaded with hula hoops, balls, jump ropes, bean bags, and Buzz Glass records. Oh, yes. I needed students. Our blind and visually impaired specialist provided my with several referrals as did our deaf and partial hearing teachers. I knew that as soon as parents were aware of a new service I would become overwhelmed with students to evaluate, schedule, and service. I was ready.

One of my first students was Chris F. He attended a K through eight school in his home town of Penryn, a small town about seven miles west of Auburn. Chris was born premature and was given high doses of pure oxygen. The treatment may have saved his life, but left him with a condition known as retrolental fibroplasia (RLF). He had some vision as an infant, but was soon totally blind. He was a sandy haired intelligent boy of six when I first met him. His parents insisted that he attend school with his peers, where he had the splendid help of the county Vision Specialist, Lynn. She taught him mobility, provided braille texts, books on tape, and counseled his classroom teachers. Chris was learning cane walking, but seldom used it at school. He was comfortable with having a classmate guide by allowing him to lightly hold an elbow while walking one step behind. He asked his guide to describe the surroundings. His personality and openness led to full acceptance in the school. To the students and teachers of Penryn Chris was just another student. His parents were very involved and were pioneering the least restrictive environment clause in the county. The alternative was a state school for the blind in the Bay Area.

Lynn introduced me to Chris during my first week with students. Twenty years later Chris attended my retirement party as a twenty-six-year-old young adult.

I took Chris from his class for a half an hour each week. He was usually ready and anxious not to miss a minute. The Sacramento region holds an annual "Blind Olympics" and Chris always participated. I gave him pointers in running with a leader. He would run beside me while lightly holding a small lope of webbing as I explained the surroundings to him. One morning, when we were practicing for the long jump, I had Chris feel the take-off rubber, pace back to the start, turn, run counting steps, and leap forward. He became so excited after one successful jump that he turned left instead of right as we had practiced and he smashed his head into the playground swings. The sound was like a pumpkin hitting concrete. He fell to the ground as a huge lump grew on his noggin. I felt horrible for not protecting him. I took him to the lunchroom, got a bag of ice for the head, filled out an accident report, and called his mother. Chris's only reaction, "I'm okay, let's not stop the practice." His mom said, "Hey it happens all the time. I don't want him afraid to move." Got to love the attitude.

Chris was my only student at Penryn. We would begin with a warm up and perhaps a light run around the grass playground. I was given a playground ball with a bell inside by Lynn and Chris could field the rolled "bell" ball or kick it after locating it by sound. He learned to throw correctly with voice instruction. I would move four or five steps left or right. "Here Chris," I would shout, and he eventually learned to throw a ball or bean bag waist high toward the sound, first from five feet, then from up to twenty. Chris loved to show classmates his new found skills. He knew all his peers and most of the staff by their voice. "Hey, Melody, watch me throw a ball." His friends loved his enthusism. He learned to catch a regulation eight and one half inch ball if I bounced it. As his skill level improved he could move left or right a step or two to catch the bounced ball that he located by the bounce sound. We also worked on his body awareness, balance, and position in space. I would throw bean bags on the playground then ask Chris to find them while I gave direction. "Two steps left," or "four feet in front of you," until he found all the objects. I was occasionally able to bring a classmate to work with Chris. I would instruct his friend how to properly throw to Chris and asked the helper to play ball with Chris at recess or during their PE class. Peer tutors worked really well in this instance. At times I had a small group of his friends work with Chris. We sometimes played a game of "blind man's bluff." This gave Chris a rare advantage over his classmates. Lynn was working with Chris attempting to rid him of some "blindisms" such as shaking his head side to side. Think of Ray Charles. He would also make noises that were inappropriate. I tried to help in this regard. Chris didn't have the feedback that sighted children have in order to modify their behavior to be socially acceptable. I found it difficult to separate gentle reminders from outright nagging.

Chris taught me about perception. He was very willing to talk about his blindness. He told me that he understood colors; red meant hot, blue cold, white was ice, or green was soft grass. He would touch a relief map to feel hills and mountains. He attended movies with his friends and loved to travel with his parents. In short, Chris lived as a normal six-year-old boy. Hopes and aspirations were the same. He said to me, "I'd like to be able to see, but I don't know what that is." I would continue to work with Chris during his years at Penryn. He did spend some summer school time at the School for the Blind in order to learn special skills and take advantage of the technology and unique curriculum that they provide. However, he always returned to his classmates in his small school.

I was able to counsel Chris' teachers about adapting activities so he could more fully and successfully participate in regular PE classes. Balance and basic movement skills are essential in first grade but are seldom taught. I presented his teacher with materials from my mentors Jack Capon and Buzz Glass so that the entire class was practicing jumping, hopping, skipping, catching, throwing, and basic balance. It was my hope that having Chris in the class improved the movement activities for all his classmates.

Chris and I worked together throughout his elementary schooling. While in the sixth grade, his parents asked if I could help him with physical fitness. We did a brief warm up each session, but not much more than a few minutes. One of his goals was to run five kilometers (three point one miles). It is difficult for blind children to develop fitness and Chris was getting pretty soft. We started with small jogs around the playground for two minutes and gradually progressed, leaving the school grounds and running the back roads of Penryn. Chris worked his way up to over four miles by the spring. I wanted him to enter a local race and I would pace him, but he didn't feel the need for that. I told Chris about a blind acquaintance of mine named Harry Cordelleos. I met Harry while running the Catalina Marathon. Harry ran over a hundred-fifty marathons, several ultramarathons, snow skied, played golf, once water skied twenty-six miles, and wrote a book about his adventures called, "No Limits." Chris was inspired, but not overly motivated. A good friend of mine suggested that I should take a photo of Harry and me. "Why should I do that Lisa?" I asked. "So you can show it to Chris, of course," she replied. I had to gently reminder her that Chris was blind. "Oh yeah," she said, "I forgot."

In high school Chris worked for a small technology firm helping to test and develop software for the blind, played in the marching band, and maintained top grades. He was then and remains today an inspiration to all who know him.

One Tuesday morning, I packed my car, headed fifty miles east over Donner Summit on Highway 80 and met with Martin, the Special Ed Director of the Tahoe Truckee School

District. He wanted me to work in five schools in the district each week. There were children in each school with active IEPs. I began in Truckee Elementary school. The chain smoking principal introduced me to three children, a seven-year-old girl with Down syndrome, a nine-year-old boy with mild Cerebral Palsy, and a ten-year-old boy with serious behavioral problems. They were mine for a half hour. Each had different needs and skill levels. We were able to work together on balance, catching and throwing games. They loved throwing bean bags at Styrofoam bowling pins and watching them topple to the floor. I merely changed the distance each child threw to even their chances. Once more, my boy with the severe behavioral issues enjoyed tutoring the younger children. Behavior was seldom a problem for me because the kids usually loved, if not my activities, being out of their classrooms. They often called me the play teacher. I accepted that.

North Tahoe School had a great view of Lake Tahoe. I worked with the severely handicapped class (SH) that I had applied to teach five years prior. Jan, the teacher, was at a loss when it came to PE. I was able to help her develop activities for her children. Mobility was a real problem for her class as they had several flights of stairs to climb between playground and classroom. Luckily none of her children were in wheelchairs, but several had crutches and impaired gaits. We worked on balance activities and had games that involved gross motor movements. I would leave work sheets for Jan to follow and for the most part she did. Fitness was vital for her SH students. They needed to work on flexibility as well. I had only one half hour a week with Jan's class, so without her cooperation gains would be minimal.

After a visit to three Lake Tahoe Schools, I returned to Truckee and worked with one of my most challenging students. His name was Jorden, a nine-year-old boy who had been in a serious automobile accident. Both his parents had been killed and Jorden had lost his right arm, suffered head trauma, and was partially paralyzed on the left side. He had essentially one functioning limb, his right leg. He wore an arm prosthesis, but had little function with it. Jorden lived with his grandparents who were very concerned with his well-being. He carried deep emotional scars from losing his parents and from the physical trauma. Jorden needed lots of positive feedback. We played a slow game of kickball working on kicking with the right leg while maintaining balance with the left. After a few sessions I saw steady improvement and more willingness to attempt new skills. Jorden was beginning to actually have fun during physical activities. When we were observed by some of his classmates they were encouraging. "Way to go Jorden, nice kick," they would yell. We began catching by rolling a ball on a cafeteria table while he was in a sitting position, thus the ball was always on the same level and he could easily push it back to me. We eventually worked without the help of a table and Jorden was able to trap a thrown Nerf ball against his body and then push it forward using his prosthetic hand and his somewhat immobile left arm. He was subject to falls and wore a helmet when on the playground. Progress was slow for Jorden, but it was steady. His grandmother became a bit less protective of him.

Unfortunately, I was not able to convince his teachers that he could participate in the regular PE activities. PE at Truckee was unique because they had a regular cross-country ski program at the school. Jorden and I were able to "walk" together on skis during the winter months, which in Truckee lasted well into the spring. In the summer, Jorden was enrolled in the PH school program in Newcastle, and I became his summer school teacher. He and grandmother stayed with relatives for the summer in nearby Auburn.

I worked in the Tahoe area schools for the first two years as their APE Specialist. At Tahoe Lake Elementary, I met an enthusiastic PE teacher named Jill who was very interested in developing a district Adapted PE Program. She eventually took over my caseload and I no longer had to make the hundred twenty mile-round trip to the Lake. I loved the area as a playground in the summer but not when the howling winter winds blew down from the mountains. I thought I would be able to spend time on the trails near Donner Summit after teaching for the day, but seldom had the good weather or energy to do so. This area often has the deepest snow in the lower forty-eight. Oddly enough the only time I missed a session at Tahoe-Truckee was in early June because of snow. Go figure.

In October of my first APE year, I attended the annual conference on Adapted Physical Education held each year in California. It took place in conjunction with CAHPERD (California Association for Health Physical Education Recreation and Dance). This for me was a break-out experience because I was for the first time among other APE specialists. I had felt like I was flying solo before. I quickly learned that no two programs were alike. The large city school specialists often had a gym to themselves and had the children brought to them. They saw the children twice a week and did little driving. Rural teachers were itinerant, stretched thin, were flexible with workspace, and carried portable equipment. Each position had its' challenges. I naturally gravitated toward the sessions on rural issues. I became close with Dave and Larry, APE specialists from nearby Nevada County. They had been at the job for several years and had realistic answers to my abundant questions. They had developed a placement procedure utilizing standard testing. To qualify for APE services a student must have special needs not met by the regular PE program, and must fall within the lower fifth percentile in physical performances such as balance, movement, or ball skills. Dave had a template prepared for report writing which I exploited. I made a point of attending this conference yearly, often with Dave and Larry. We even once flew to the conference in a private plane piloted by the mayor of Nevada City. The sessions were full of activities and games, and would you believe, I even met my old mentor Buzz Glass at one. He had retired from Oakland and was now presenting workshops and demonstrations for the love of the subject with little or no remuneration.

In the late summer of my first year, I was able to attend a week long PE workshop at Cal Poly in San Luis Obispo accompanied as usual by Dave and Larry. Again it was a very informative seminar and provided me with even more ammunition for my classes. The classes were not specifically attuned to Adapted PE, but we found our APE colleagues easily. On the last day of the workshop there was a five K run. I looked around the several hundred participants and though I would do well. I did, except I hadn't taken into account the high school track coaches. I got crushed by them.

In spite of workshops and conferences, I still did not have the clear APE credential and felt uneasy about my lack of formal training. The State Department of Education was beginning to tighten up on grandfathered credentials. My boss emphatically suggested that I get the clear credential. The University of the Pacific in Stockton ran a summer credential program, but the cost was high and I needed to work summer school. I therefore chose to attend Sacramento State night classes to win the coveted piece of paper. **The APE designation was usually added to an existing Physical Education credential. I enrolled in the fall term at Sacramento State to begin the process. I would be able to complete the required courses in two semesters. I drove to Sacramento two nights a week. I was the oldest in the classes, and was often looked up to because I was actually teaching in the area that other students were just beginning to pursue. Twice during the fall semester, I filled in for absent professors. I found the kinesiology class particularly difficult. Most of the students were in the pre-physical therapy program and it was assumed that all had a working background of physiology and anatomy. I had neither. I blew the mid-term, however, so did about sixty percent of the students. Other classes were easy because they covered issues that I was dealing with daily. I often thought the instructors had little idea of the daily life of** an Adapted PE teacher especially in a rural setting, but I held my tongue. After completing two semesters of work, and receiving good grades, all of the required courses for the credential were completed. I had to apply through the University's Physical Education Department for a recommendation for the credential. It was denied by Dr. Whitmore, the head of the department! What? I stormed into her office and demanded to know why I was denied. She was one of the professors for whom I had subbed. Her reasoning, "Why should I recommend you for a placement that my four year students should have, and you don't even have a regular physical education credential." She was immovable in that regard. I returned to the office of Jeannie Bartell, who had agreed that I could be grandfathered into the job. She said my only recourse was to challenge the PE credential by passing the National Standard PE test. If passed, it would allow me to apply for the PE credential and add the APE designation to it, thus bypassing Sacramento State. I agreed. Took the test. Passed it in the ninety-fifth percentile and finally had a clear credential to do what I had been doing for over two years. Blahh, jumping through hoops was not amusing.

Things were beginning to sort themselves out at home. I moved from my apartment into a house that Wendy and I had as a rental. Tuesday nights were still Dawn and Dad nights and she spent every other weekend with me. Wendy's cancer was in remission, and she seemed to be settling in to her new life as well. One afternoon I received a call from Dawn's kindergarten teacher. She said she just had to call me. My anxiety rose like a Saturn B rocket. What was wrong? She was stifling a laugh. "Well, I asked my class if anyone knew a song that they could share with the class," she said. Precocious Dawn raised her hand as usual, went to the front of the class, and sang, "Poisoning Pigeons in the Park" by Tom Lehrer. She proudly told her classmates, "My daddy taught it to me."

"What can I say? Dawn shares my sense of the ridiculous," I sheepishly said.

"Well," Dawn's teacher said, "the two of you made my day." No harm no foul.

Running became my comfort and my social outlet. I graduated from the marathon distance and tested the waters of an ultra-marathon. I had paced at Western States and done the High Sierra Three Step, so I cheerfully entered the American River Fifty miler. The race meandered from Sacramento to Auburn much of it on trails that I knew well. I could see no reason why I couldn't run the race in under eight hours. Race day I found several reasons. Cramps and a foot injury equaled "a did not finish" (DNF). I ran forty miles, but was unable to continue. Disappointed? Yes, but not done with Ultras. On Wednesday nights I met with a small group of runners, male and female, fast and slow, beginners and veterans. We ran six to ten miles from a city park, from various members' homes, or from a local pizza parlor. This gang of amateur athletes became my clan. Some of us would meet on weekends and run together on the trails that Auburn is so blessed with. Throughout the years we became known as the Sierra Express Running Club. We were an eclectic group including, a doctor, a dentist (Fat Jack), a judge, construction workers, janitors, lawyers, policemen, and even a teacher or two. We socialized, shared accomplishments, and suffered defeats, together. Our friendships remained strong even after our bodies turned on us.

Perhaps my favorite school was in the snug foothill town of Foresthill. It is a twenty mile trip on a winding forest road from the main highway. The town is a throwback to another era, with a small main street, several don't dare enter bars, a timber mill, and a small school. The K through eight school sat between two branches of the American River surrounded by forest. The staff was laid back, jeans wearing, and involved with the community. It had a high percentage of male teachers including at the kindergarten level. I felt more welcome there than in the larger suburban schools. I scheduled Foresthill Elementary at the end of the day on Thursdays. I usually brought my running clothes so I could get some training in on the Western States trail that ran through town.

The Resource Teacher at Foresthill, Elaine became my go-to contact. She asked if I would like to present a PE workshop for the elementary staff. I was happy to do so. After school one Thursday I cancelled my run and met with most, if not all, of the kindergarten through sixth grade teachers. I gave pointers about an effective and inexpensive elementary school PE program. A movement program is essential and can be incorporated into academic areas. PE is not sports or coaching. It is teaching just as much as reading or math. PE equipment is NOT recess equipment where there is often one ball for twenty children and the most proficient students will dominate. Those who need the practice most will get the least. Baseball is a no-no for small children. I got in big trouble because of this statement (sorry Little League parents). It has little or no aerobic value, pits the most skilled player (usually the pitcher) against the least skilled and requires a high skill level to perform. Remember trying to catch a ground ball? Soccer is a much better replacement. I showed the teachers how they could have an effective PE program without costly equipment, a gym, or even a playground. I also presented them with a list of games and activities that permit movement for the whole class. Some were mine, others I got from books or workshops. I was heartened to see my ideas catch on and was able to witness elementary classes playing new and full participation games, like "Elves, Giants, and Wizards." I was often asked PE questions by the staff and would present them with more material as I developed it. I gave workshops for other schools, but seldom received the positive response that I did in Foresthill.

A typical Foresthill student was Blue Sky. He lived in a nearby canyon with no electricity, had never played with a ball, but climbed rocks and trees with abandon. Blue was reluctant to participate in PE with his class and he tested low enough for inclusion into my APE program. Blue quickly learned to throw, catch, and kick. He was dismissed from my PE program after a few months. As the regulations became more refined, Blue would not have been eligible for APE. I was happy to work with him at the time, however, and believed that the sessions made a difference to his sense of self-worth.

There were others with more pressing needs. Tom was a sixth grader with hemophilia. He often had large bruises on his limbs from internal bleeding and was in need of a protective environment, hence was excluded from PE with his class. I worked with him in a small group of younger children. We used soft balls to prevent injury. Tom had the requisite PE skills so he was used as a role model for other children in the small group. His parents moved from Foresthill so that Tom could be closer to a major medical center.

Angie was a third grader confined to a motorized chair and lived with spastic Cerebral Palsy. She was a slight girl with blonde hair and expressive eyes. Her charm was in her "I can do it" attitude. She had limited speech, all four limbs were involved, and yet she thrived in her class. She was able to throw a bean bag but not a large ball. Her IEP goals were to improve mobility in her chair and utilizing her upper body for gross motor skills. Angie learned to throw and hit a target, could move her chair through an obstacle course, and maneuver over rough ground. I took Tom, Angie, and several other students on brief walks in the forest trails behind the school. We would examine trees, insects, and flowers as well as share our feelings about nature. PE? I think so. Recreation and appreciation of the surrounding wilderness was vital to all students.

Auburn had five elementary schools and one middle school. One entire day, therefore, was spent there. It was a full day, but had little travel. EV Caine, the middle school, was my early morning assignment. I had a small group of six boys. Including some from a PCOE special class. Brian was a boy I had worked with at the PH school. He was a no quit sports loving boy with moderate CP. He and the other five students loved watching football and were avid Forty-Niner fans. I reinvented football so they could all participate. We used a soft football and set up a grid on the playground of about twenty-by-fifteen yards. I gave my receivers a pattern to run, while the defenders attempted to intercept the ball and/or touch the passer; me. If a player didn't have the skill to actually catch, he only had to get his hands on the ball and it was a reception (Jerry Rice eat your heart out). Once the ball was "caught" the play was dead. Ten yards for a first down, ten more for a touchdown. The boys loved spiking the ball after a score. We talked about rules of the "real" game so they could better enjoy watching it on TV or in person at the local high schools. This group was my most advanced class of the day and they took their games very seriously. As the year wore on we moved to hockey, soccer, basketball, and other modified team sports. I looked forward to seeing them each week. One of my most likable students was a part of this group. Keith was a special class student who needed extra encouragement in physical skills. I never had a diagnosis for his lack of ability. He was an "FLK"; forgive the un-PC term meaning "funny looking kid." When I asked Keith a question he often would look at me confused and say, "I can't know." The truth is he often just couldn't know.

At EV Cain one Tuesday, I received a note in my mailbox. A PE instructor who I knew only in passing asked to see me. I met her after school that day. "Gene, can you take a look at one of my students?" she asked.

I replied of course, but wanted to know what she was concerned about.

"I have a lovely seventh grade girl who is walking weird." She said.

I explained to her that I could screen the girl, but would need a formal referral through the Special Ed. administrator before I could do any formal testing and only after an IEP could I enroll her in my program. Many children, particularly those in middle school, have strange walks. She understood, but I felt her genuine apprehension.

The following week, I made time to observe Jenny during her PE period. Indeed, her balance was poor. She seemed to have to think carefully before placing one foot in front of the other. I also noticed that Jenny tired easily and had a slight tremble in her hands. She was otherwise a normal appearing seventh grade girl, with a blonde swinging ponytail and soft blue eyes. Assuming Jenny had a medical problem, I contacted the school nurse who was not aware of Jenny's condition. She observed Jenny and she too was troubled with her unusual gait. It was her role in the process to contact the parents. They assumed that Jenny just had the usual growing pains and the awkwardness of a preteen girl, but would take her to their GP for a physical. At that point, I had a formal referral for Jenny that allowed me to test her. She fell in the lower fifth percentile in balance and lower body gross motor skills. She didn't have the coordination to kick a ball with any but the weakest impact. I also noted poor muscle tone and the noticeable tremor. I asked her if she had seen her doctor. "Yeah, and he sent me to a nerve specialist," Jenny said.

"What did he say?" I asked.

"Well, he told my parents I've got some kind of ataxia."

I knew that was just a general term for poor balance, but that was already established. I was able to enroll Jenny in my weekly APE program.

When I next saw her, she told me her neurologist called her parents with the diagnosis of Friedreich's Ataxia. I had never heard of that disorder but went on a computer that evening and my breath was taken from me. The disease is found in one in fifty thousand people in the United States. It is a degenerative disease with no known cure and will eventually involve all limbs, the spine, heart, the senses, and usually leads to an early death. That girl was in for a long tough struggle without a happy ending. I was personally heartbroken. She was such a sweet intelligent girl.

I worked with Jenny for two years and saw the regrettable progression of her disease and her downward spiral. During her eighth grade, I worked with her one-on-one. She was in a motorized chair, had difficulty with speech, and her breathing was becoming labored. Her IEP included, speech therapy, occupational therapy, and my Adapted PE. Jenny and I would often meet in the school library and play table and board games. She loved to read and we would discuss her favorite author, Joseph Kellerman. I was doing more counseling than PE, but Jenny needed to sometimes vent. She was upbeat most of the time, even when her parents got on her case as her grades began to decline. In the following years, I would occasionally see Jenny motoring in her chair after high school let out. I would pull my car over so we could have a talk. Her attitude was still strong even as her body wasted away. I lost contact with Jenny after her high school days, but often think of her as the sweet girl I met so long ago.

After two years of establishing the Adapted PE program for the county, I had been too successful. I had an unmanageable caseload of over seventy students, not including my occasional sessions with PCOE special classes. My supervisors agreed that another APE specialist was necessary. That summer Lila and I interviewed several worthy candidates. One stood out and we hired Pam K. She had a "mother-earth" personality, was an experienced PE teacher, had taught overseas, and seemed to be a warm and concerned person. She brought not only welcome relief to me but new ideas and outlooks. I found it difficult to give up some of my chargers but was happy to have a partner who understood the difficulties and joys of the job. We split the county districts, Pam handling most of the western end and the more suburban areas, while I continued with the eastern side and the more rural schools. Pam had her own ideas of how to run a program, but we were essentially in agreement and had a good working relationship that lasted until I retired.

I now had more time to help with some county special classes. Perhaps my favorite was in the small rural K-8 school in Ophir. The Ophir School was unique because, along with the regular school population, it housed the Placer County deaf and hard of hearing program. Alice T taught the preschool deaf program of children from three to five years of age. Older deaf children were integrated into the regular classes and had the assistance of sign language interpreters. In fact, most of the children in Ophir became proficient in American Sign Language. On the playground it was impossible to discern who was deaf and who was not. I had only one deaf student on my caseload at the school and only because of associative balance issues rather than his deafness. One deaf boy who I worked with briefly went on to play varsity football at Placer High School, an APE success story,

When I entered Alice's preschool class, there was applause and wide eyed joy from her students. I had only a basic understanding of sign language, but Alice was always there to help. I knew she would reinforce the skills I introduced to her kids. Some of her students had cochlear implants, others were totally deaf. One small charmer, Billy, was not deaf, but lost his ability to speak from ingesting a toxic chemical as a toddler. High fives were given to each child and we started with balance, rhythm games, and basic movement activities. Alice was convinced that movement activities were essential for her class. I arrived at her class one day and found a subdued atmosphere. Billy had succumbed to his health problems and died that week. Special Education has more than its share of heartbreaks. Alice was devastated, and I could only offer a hug and condolences.

Ophir School also provided me with one of my favorite small groups. Four students of mixed strengths were enrolled. Art, a small wheelchair bound boy with CP who had boundless enthusiasm and intelligence; Kate, who had minimal CP and the personality of a golden retriever puppy; Molly, a first grader with Down syndrome; and lastly, Davey, the deaf boy with balance difficulties. The group varied in age from six to ten, but all got along well. Art would often have a strong opinion about the activities he wanted for the week. Kate was never discouraged by her slight limp and uncooperative arm. Molly was my energizer bunny, a non-stop tornado of "let's play." Davey, while more reserved, was a full participant. One of their favorite games was bocce ball. Each had different skill sets so I would team them to make things honest and competitive. In bocce ball you didn't know the outcome until the final ball was rolled which added drama to their game. I could tease Kate by saying, "Girls can't run fast." She would answer by flying down the playground and then add, "How about that Mr. T." Point well taken, Kate.

My one faux-pas at Ophir occurred during my inaugural APE year. I wrote a report on a boy who I felt did not qualify for my program. He was severely overweight and reluctant to participate in regular Physical Education. While I understood his difficulty, he had no disability other than his weight. I was called into the principal's office. I knew I had blundered when I saw my report in his hands. "Gene, we have a problem." "That is never a good start," I thought. My report stated that the boy in question was *obese*. While true, parents will certainly take offense at that description. The principal who was obese, took exception as well. Bottom line, I rewrote the report stating that the student's weight did not match his skeletal frame. One must be PC even in PE.

The weight game came into play once again at nearby Newcastle Elementary. A fourth grade boy, Ronaldo, was referred to me because of his size. He tipped the scales at over two hundred pounds, was unable to run at all due to chronically inflamed ankles, and was pre-diabetic. I had the county school nurse, Anne, do a health assessment on him and together we marched into a late afternoon IEP meeting. Anne and I agreed that Ronaldo was not just obese but was morbidly obese, although we stated it differently. Mom and Dad, the Newcastle principal, my supervisor, his classroom teacher, Anne, Ronaldo, and I sat around a table on third grader chairs. My heart sank when I realized that only Anne and I were not seriously overweight. She and I presented the facts and all but the three hundred pound father saw the need for some intervention. Ronaldo was enrolled in my program and Mom agreed to restrict his intake of sugar and starch. Dad left in a huff, saying, "Ronaldo is just like me." He did sign the agreement, however. I helped design an exercise program for Ronaldo and had limited success, when his growth began to catch up to his weight.

Obesity is a growing problem within the school age population. While it alone would not be cause for placement into the APE program it was a major contributing factor for many of my students and one I was not successful in ameliorating. I tried to help establish a weight reduction program in Foresthill. The principal, teachers, and cafeteria staff were willing to follow some nutritional guidelines and use aerobic exercise as part of their PE activities. However, few parents were willing to jump on the band wagon, and the best intentions were soon scuttled with more academic needs. The children who were overweight often had more attitude problems than most of my students. One girl at a Roseville school was so opposed to exercise that I almost had to dismiss her because of lack of cooperation. I made a devil's agreement with her. If she worked with me for fifteen minutes, she could return to her class, but she had to really work. This seemed the only way I was able to get her to participate at all. My plan was to increase the time factor each week. Her teacher was not keen on her returning to the classroom early, and got in touch with the parents, who got in touch with the principal, who got in touch with my supervisor, who, you guessed it, got in touch with me. My uncooperative student and I struggled through the rest of the year. Things did improve the following year when I had additional classmates to work with us. She eventually found that some movement could actually be fun.

With few exceptions as noted above, discipline was seldom an issue for me. My students were having too much fun to jeopardize leaving a session. A threat to return them to their class usually was enough to calm any poor behavior. As with most good theater, I tried to leave them laughing and wanting for more at dismissal. I was sensitive to the emotional needs of the students. I didn't want them to feel that they were being pulled from their peers solely because of their disabilities. Indeed, most of their classmates would love to have participated in what they perceived as fun new games. When possible, I would involve regular more capable peers to join in some of our sessions but never at the expense of my special students.

I received a referral at Lincoln High School regarding a junior boy who had been working under his car when it fell off the blocks. He was paralyzed from the waist down and wheelchair bound. He was devastated by the trauma and the attention that it brought him. The last thing he wanted was to be separated as a "special student." He did qualify for APE services, had an IEP that his parents initiated, but was so reluctant to work with me that I had to cancel his program. I instead got the PE teachers to allow him to work in the gym on upper body conditioning, and flexibility. He was eventually given a pass from all PE participation. I was relieved not to be working in a high school again but hated the fact that a student thought that my services were more of an obstacle than a help. It reminded me of the medical oath, "First do no harm."

CHAPTER 13

ADAPTED PE THE LATER YEARS

During the first few years as the only Adapted PE Specialist, I was adjusting well to being single once again. Belonging to the Sierra Express running club brought new goals, weekly gatherings for runs and picnics, and more importantly a personal sense of satisfaction. I dated several women during these years, but nothing serious came of the relationships. Wendy recovered from her war with the cancer demon and the divorce had become finalized. Dawn often traveled with me to Saturday morning runs. She would read a book or work an aid station, then we would have breakfast afterwards. She amazed me one day ordering the "Trucker's Special" and finishing it! What a kid.

In 1982 I succumbed to temptation and put in for the Western States one hundred mile run. If I was drawn in the lottery, I would have to complete a fifty mile run in under ten hours. Luckily, I was chosen, as were four friends and we began the six months of training with long slow mountain trail runs. We joked, laughed, and wore ourselves out on the paths during the spring. We all qualified during the California Fifty, a run in Santa Rosa, CA and set our sights on the last week in June. I trained hard and averaged about ninety miles per week for the last month. With two pacers, and a crew to help and encourage me, what could go wrong? Race day temperatures topped one hundred degrees in the canyons and the allure of the silver belt buckle, representing a sub twenty-four hour finish, did me in. I threw up early and often, cramped, and began walking near my favorite school in Foresthill. Ten miles later and seventy miles into the race, I needed help just to step off a scale. A physical therapist examined my unresponsive quads and my wristband was cut signaling a DNF (Did Not Finish). I learned that hydration, electrolytes, and proper pacing would be vital in hundred mile adventures. I called my best friend and training partner, Dr. John, to congratulate him on his finish, only to find that he too went belly up. I waited two more years before testing the waters of another hundred mile race.

In 1985, I worked summer school once again. This time I was back at Secret Ravine School but due to Least Restrictive Environment clause, the school now housed only classes for the emotionally disturbed. I had a class consisting of children much like those at Camp Wediko. Looking back at the make-up, I realized that I had a number of children were functioning at the higher end of the autism spectrum, most likely with Asperger's. I initiated an exercise program first thing in the morning. We changed into gym clothes and did brief warm up calisthenics then went for a short run. I was criticized for bringing my exercise passion into the class, but the response from most of my kids was very positive. We set goals, measured progress, and I awarded medals and ribbons to all who participated. I had parental permissions for all but one boy. He worked with my aide for that period on other life skills, such as cooking, and gardening. On a field trip we hiked a portion of trail in the Auburn State Park examining the native plants and birds. It was a fun summer session.

Following summer school, I made a trip to Alaska to visit my roommate from graduate school, Gary Aanes. He was now the Deputy Director of Vocational Rehabilitation for the entire state. He told me that after graduation from Greeley, he tried to contact me, but didn't know my whereabouts. He had a job offer for me that was a custom fit. At that time, I was desperately searching for work while living in San Francisco. I'd have gone to Alaska in a heartbeat. What a different life I'd have led in the 49th State. Gary asked me to officiate at his wedding while on an Alaskan Marine Highway cruise. I was most happy to perform the ceremony on the back deck while motoring toward Prince William Sound. He and his wife Susan are still married so, "It worked."

Upon my return and before school began, I received a letter in the mail in response to a singles ad I placed in a Sacramento paper. This was before computer dating and I was not into the bar scene, so I place ads a number of times and met some very interesting women, some of whom I dated. This one was the most intriguing yet. In her return letter, Suzi Clark wrote, "If meeting someone who can run a hundred miles intimidates you, don't bother responding." Well hell, I knew many women who had run a hundred miles. My response when I called her was, "Did you buckle?" (Run sub twenty-four hours). We agreed to meet at a local trailhead after my daily run. "How will I know you? I asked. "Oh, I'll just ride in on a white horse," she said. I'll be damned if that isn't what happened. She was from nearby Folsom, was an animal health tech, knew many of the same running friends, seemed carefree and footloose, and owned a white Arabian horse named Abe.

The annual end of summer party was once again the High Sierra Three Step, a three day celebration of sporting excess. That summer was my sixth time at the event. We ran, laughed, drank beer, told numerous lies, and enjoyed camp fires while we all sang "Dead skunk in the Middle of the Road" with Rob Bonner on the guitar. Food and spirits were plentiful as we renewed friendships and had our feet mended by "Blister Mary," a local nurse. The end of the trail was at a spot called White Oak Flatt, the scene of my DNF at Western States. We could invited civilians (non-participants) to the trailside dinner. I invited Suzi and she fit right in with our close knit sweaty running group. She rode to the party once again on her white horse. Within a month, she moved into my small Auburn house along with her lovable, but blind Boston Terrier, Raisin. The horse stayed in its own stall, thank god.

After having completed the Boston Marathon and numerous fifty mile running events, I had nothing left to prove other than having another go at the holy grail of Ultra running, a hundred mile run. With Suzi's enthusiasm overcoming my reluctance, I signed up for the Wasatch Front one hundred mile run. It was a formidable challenge, more difficult than Western States, but had a thirty-six hour time limit instead of the Western States' thirty. Due to poor planning on my part, I lost ten pounds in the first twenty-five miles, but managed to punish myself and pushed toward the finish line in Midway, Utah. I walked much more than I ran through the long cold night. I vowed not to quit again as long as I remained moving forward. (Thus my poem, The Quitter) I took great satisfaction with my thirty-one hour finish, even though it wasn't pretty. It was my slowest time of my eleven hundred mile finishes, but I beat the demon, I could go the distance.

I got a new personal license plate—ULTRAPE. Ultra because I was running ultras, and APE as an Adapted PE specialist. Made sense to me, until a principal approached me. She said, "Gene, do you realize that your license plate could be interpreted as ultimate rape." Wow that one got by me. I went to the Department of Motor Vehicles and changed it the next day, before anyone else noted the interpretation.

My other passion was travel. I couldn't put aside a lecture from my geography teacher at Keene State. Oddly enough, it was Miss Keene who spoke with passion of her trip to Peru. In graphic detail, she recalled looking down on Machu Picchu from the Sun Gate as the early morning light illuminated the ancient city of stone. I needed to see this for myself. I saved my pennies throughout the teaching year and summer school. In August, Suzi and I landed in Lima, Peru amid warnings that the Shining Path terrorists were a genuine threat. Lima was under martial law, and we were frightened just walking around the city even in the daylight. We felt safer in Cusco, and other than a bout of food poisoning, I loved the ancient Inca city and the nearby Sacred Valley. We hiked the Inca trail in three days and I relived Miss Keene's story as we passed the Sun Gate and stared down through the morning haze toward Machu Picchu. I was in awe by the majesty of the Peruvian Andes. They soared well over twenty thousand feet and I was enchanted. I needed to return and climb these cathedrals in the sky.

We returned in time to run the High Sierra Three Step together this time. Then it was back to reality and life behind the windshield as an Adapted PE Specialist once more.

I found the most difficult weeks of the year are the first two. I always had new students to test, to report on, and to prepare IEPs for. In addition, I had to talk to teachers and prepare a schedule. This was often like herding cats. I needed to fit in about sixty students in twenty schools onto a matrix that worked around travel time, recesses, lunches, arrival, and dismissal times. Most teachers understood my restrictions and limitations, but a few were insistent that I not take their students during academic classes. I tried to accommodate them as much as possible, but often it was not possible. If push came to shove, I called the parents and let them be the arbitrator. We usually came to some compromise.

One fall morning in Roseville, I was with my student on the playground while he was at recess. A gentleman approached me and asked, "Who are you?"

My reply was, "I am Mr. Thibeault, the Adapted PE instructor here and who are you?"

He looked confused, but said, "I'm Mr. Sherman, the principal." Whoops, I had not done my homework. Teachers, aides, and school yard assistants often questioned the presence of this strange man at "their" school. I was sometimes asked to sign in before going on campus and occasionally to sign out as well. Two other schools asked me to stop in the office and wear a visitor badge. These annoyances, I understood, but they took time away from working with students. Once again I tried to seek some accommodations that didn't take time from my kids, but as school security became more of a priority, especially after Nine-Eleven, this task became more difficult.

I was assigned to the two schools, in the rural Placer Hills district. I had only one student, John, at the Sierra Hills Elementary School in 1986. He was a shy boy and refused to participate in physical activates, often walking with his head down and hands in his pockets. He was in the Resource Program, so was eligible for APE. While approaching the school early one morning, traffic was unusually backed up. I feared that I would be late for my student and that would put the whole day's schedule off track. I inched toward the school and spotted the reason for the hold up. There had been a serious traffic accident blocking the two lane road into Meadow Vista, and it was just in the process of being cleared. Once through the traffic, I rushed to John's class, only to have his teacher motion me into the hall. "There has been an accident," she said with a look of anguish on her face. "John's mother was seriously injured, John, his brother, and the baby are in the hospital." I was shocked to say the least. The next day I called the school to check on the condition of John and his family. His mother had died, his brother Jerry had a serious spine injury, John and the baby survived with only bruises. John was dismissed from APE at the end of the school year. Jerry, his brother, however, was on my caseload for seven years.

Jerry was in the first grade when the accident occurred. He suffered a high lumber spinal injury and was paralyzed from the lower portion of his waist down. Unlike his older brother, Jerry was upbeat, a good student, and a skilled athlete. He was the kind of student every APE teacher covets. His skills in his wheelchair were remarkable. He had to be stopped from popping wheelies on the playground, from flying in the hallways, and from giving other students thrilling rides. Throughout my years with Jerry, we played all the games that his regular PE classes were participating in. I made sure that he was fully included in his regular PE in addition to his weekly APE. In seventh grade I had to restrain him from leaping out of his chair and diving on the pavement to catch balls. He had great upper body strength, partly due to his manipulating his chair up the steep ramps at the Weimar Hills Middle School. I had taken Jerry as far as I could by the seventh grade. He could hit a tennis ball with skill, play golf, hockey, was a goalie in soccer, and was faster in his chair than most of his classmates on their good legs. After he was dismissed, Jerry was playing wheelchair basketball and tennis in an adult league and was more than holding his own against men twice his age.

PE, in general, has more than its share of accidents and APE was no exception. One morning at a Roseville school I was working with an overzealous third grade boy, Paul with Asperger's Syndrome. We worked in the cafeteria which unfortunately had its share of obstacles. My good natured student slipped on the floor and slammed has head into the corner of a table. Blood spouted from a wound in his scalp and pooled on the floor like a rising tide. I ran to the boy's restroom and tried to halt the bleeding with paper towels. Paul was dazed, but was able to walk slowly to the office where the office staff applied some needed first aid and called his Mom. I felt awful, but his mother more than understood that accidents happen, especially to her rambunctious son. He did not require any stitches and was not concussed. The next week we were ready to roll once again.

In an Auburn School, I worked with a young girl who had brittle bone disease or osteogenisis imperfecta. Kathy often had a cast on one limb or another due to fractures. Her spirit was as amazing as her body was weak. She was a good student in a special class, but was behind her peers due to missing so much school. I worked with her for a number of years, usually in small group settings. One morning we were using colored plastic spots the size of dinner plates. The game was a movement and memory activity. One student would place a colored spot on the floor. The next student had to step on it, then put another down. Each student in turn had to step on the spots in sequence then add another colored spot. Kathy tripped while stepping from one spot to the next. I didn't allow her to jump like the other children did. There was a soft crack and Kathy collapsed on the pavement with another leg fracture. My bad. Again her mother was called, an accident report was filled out, and I left feeling frustrated. I called her mother that night. Kathy was in another cast and would miss more school. Her mom just said, "Welcome to our life." Kathy was enrolled in my program for several more years without incident and I always tried to guard her without restricting her movements. I even had Kathy in a class with a blind girl which really tested my ability to protect her, but all went well.

Frequently, there is psychological pain to deal with as well as physical. A third grader named Benny in an Auburn School, had recently been diagnosed with Duchene Muscular Dystrophy. His disease progressed rapidly from a stumbling walk, to crutches, to a regular wheelchair, to an electric chair. Benny was with a varied group of three children when he noticed someone riding a bike near the school. Tears poured down his red cheeks and anger flashed like a beacon from his face. "I used to ride my bike. Now I have to sit in this f*cking chair," he lashed out in my direction. I involved the other two kids in a game and took Benny for a walk. I let him vent, but he was inconsolable. His rage was understandable, but I had no remedies for his frustrations other than empathy. I talked with his teacher and she had seen Benny lash out frequently. Professional counseling with Benny and his family had already begun with limited success. I supposed that I was more amazed that most of my MD students—I had five or six—were not angry. One became the vice president of his high school class, another was always smiling, excited, and interested in learning. Benny eventually moved on to high school and became part of a memorable session.

Along with Benny, this Auburn Elementary school group included two other boys. One had mild CP and walked with a slight limp, but was otherwise able-bodied. The second boy was a third grader who had cancer that was in remission. I asked Jason, the boy with mild CP, to run the length of the playground with the others one morning. He looked at me and sputtered, "Don't you know I'm handicapped." I looked at him with incredulity. "Don't you ever use that as an excuse. You can do whatever you set your mind to do," I lashed back at him. Unfortunately, his mother was overprotective, but I wasn't and he was the least disabled boy in the group. The other boy was Scott. He was a sparkplug of a kid, with an attitude. I kept mistakenly calling him Chris, because I had a running friend named Chris Scott, and my mind just couldn't get Scott's name right. Every time I blundered and called, "Nice kick, Chris," he would bristle and shout, "I'm Scott, not any damn Chris." I had trouble with names throughout my teaching and started to all call boys Bubba. The girls were Bubbetts. It worked for me and they seemed to like it.

I had a late afternoon class of orthopedically impaired students at Del Oro High School which included Benny. We were on an athletic field playing an adapted wheelchair game of football. I threw passes with a nerf football and the boys "ran" patterns or tried to intercept my passes. One boy loved to call the game. "Jason is going deep, he caught it for a TD, and the crowd goes wild," he broadcasted. It was a fun game and even hard to handle Benny got involved. I looked up from our game and noticed the Del Oro High football team standing near us on their way to practice. These athletes were the local heroes for my children. Joe Montana himself would have gotten no more respect than they did. The fully dressed football players were cheering my guys. "Way to go Jeremy," said one. "Nice move Benny," said another. The coach came by and gave his boys time to cheer mine. I later thanked him because it meant so much to my kids. He, in turn, said his team was inspired by my boys. It was one of those "Rudy moments" that every APE teacher yearns for.

I spent the summer of 1987 teaching a class for the severely impaired. This was the SH class with the oldest students. I'd taught summer school in many different areas of Special Ed., but this was the most difficult for me. Several of the students were bedridden, only a few were mobile, almost none were verbal. I had the expertise of two experienced aides, but felt overwhelmed. Feeding and toileting the kids was very difficult emotionally for me, but the aides took everything in stride, even dealing with an eighteen-year-old's diaper. One of the boys could only be feed through a stomach tube, another had to be suctioned to keep from choking. Each day with that class was an effort. While combing one student's hair, he turned suddenly, bit me drawing blood. My aides insisted that I call his mother because they were worried that he may have had hepatitis. I did and all I got from his mother was a scolding. "What did you do to MAKE him bite you?" she asked. I have a special respect for the teachers who deal with these classes year after year. It was not a job for me.

When that summer school ended, I headed to Mount Rainier for a week long seminar on mountaineering. I loved the course and had as a guide Eric Simonson, a Rainier Mountain Guide who would later lead many climbers to the top of Mount Everest. A group of twelve participants learned glacial travel with crampons, crevasse rescue, self-arrest with ice ax, rope handling, and other essential mountaineering skills. During the last two days of the course, we attempted the fourteen thousand foot Mount Rainier. Six of us made the summit in a whiteout. After the long down-climb, I was honored to buy a beer for Gumbu, a Sherpa, who not only accompanied Jim Whittaker to the top of Mount Everest, but was the first man to summit the mountain twice.

That fall, there was only one student of mine at the Weimar Hills Middle School. He was absent one day, and I took the free half hour to follow a *"home for sale by owner* "sign. It led me to a new house that was near completion. There was a young man doing some finishing work in the kitchen. I asked if the owner was available. "I am the owner," he replied. I was intrigued. Suzi and I were getting along well and were ready to move on to a new home. That afternoon we drove to Weimar. Suzi thought the home was special. It sat on two wooded acres among a hundred ponderosa pines. I wanted it, and put my small Auburn home for sale. I made an offer that was contingent on the sale of the Auburn home. Everything fell into line and we soon moved into the Weimar home even though it was a financial stretch. Once again Dawn would have her own room for our weekends together. She had been doing very well in school and developed a talent for speech contests. Over the years she won local and state wide competitions. Her delighted dad was usually more nervous than she was.

That December I was drawn to enter the Western States one hundred mile race once more. This was an opportunity to redeem my DNF from my previous attempt at this highly competitive event. I spent many weekends running with friends on the trails around Auburn and Foresthill. In that spring I ran three fifty mile races in five weeks and felt prepared. The race went well and I ran into the Placer High School stadium in a time of twenty-two hours, twenty minutes, with my friend and running partner Dr. John screaming, "silver, silver." Indeed I was rewarded with the Silver under twenty-four hour buckle. I had arrived as an ultra-runner. After running all day and most of the night Saturday and being up until late Sunday, I still was able to limp into summer school Monday morning. After summer school, I went to Bolivia and joined a mountain climbing expedition. With the assistance of notable guides, I was able to reach another goal by climbing to over twenty-one thousand feet on Mount Illimani. I returned home in time for Suzi and me to join friends for our wedding. It was quite a momentous summer!

The school year brought changes. As always there were more schools for Pam and I to cover and I also became a mentor teacher. I somehow found time in my schedule to help a handful of PCOE special class teachers with their physical education programs as a mentor. I visited the classes and demonstrated games and activities to further physical fitness. I gave those teachers who chose to participate worksheets with program suggestions. Several teachers really bought into the program and noted considerable improvement with their class's attitude and performance. One girl in a Roseville special class always wore a frilly and inappropriate "little princess" dress. A sit up was not only a frightening concept, but was totally impossible for her. Within a month, however, she loved the exercise program and couldn't wait to demonstrate twenty sit-ups in one minute, still in her girly dress. I found the mentor program satisfying but very time consuming. There was an extra stipend for the work, but I didn't continue after my mentor year was finished.

Budgets were always an issue so I found ways to utilize simple materials. I bought a half dozen three foot long half inch dowels. I rounded off the sharp ends and painted them in three stripes of basic colors—red, yellow, and blue. They cost less than twenty dollars, provided three or four sessions of games, and they lasted for years. Some examples of my dowel games were:

1) Catch the stick with two hands, one hand, on the blue, etc.

2) Demonstrate some sports that use a stick—golf, baseball, hockey, pool, etc.

3) Balance the dowel on the back of your hand, on your shoe, on your finger, etc.

4) (My favorite) facing a partner hold the stick on the ground with one finger. When I clap, run and catch your partner's stick while he/she catches yours.

5) Move the stick around your body at the waist, knees, ankles, etc.

6) Jump over your stick, over the red, jump over the blue and turn before you land. The activities go on and on. I acquired a large assortment of balls, bean bags, balloons, scarfs for juggling, hula hoops, empty liter plastic bottles, used tennis balls from a local racket club, and many inventive supplies. Pam and I shared materials that were more

expensive such as plastic hockey sticks, or parachutes. We had a storage closet near our office and made a weekly run to reload our cars.

I still was not supplied with a computer at the office, so I set one up at my home and did most of the paper work there. Our secretary, Sam, was suffering from being overworked and was in poor health, so she welcomed my writing reports. I developed templates for the reports which saved time and usually worked well for me. I would cut and paste parts of the narratives from year to year. This lead to a very embarrassing problem with a Foresthill student. I mistakenly misdiagnosed a student. He had Spina-bifida not Cerebral Palsy as I reported. The parents were very upset and I was reprimanded by the school psychologist. The next year I cut and pasted from the old paper and, you guessed it, I made the same mistake as the previous year. I was not present at either of the meetings so I went to the parents' home after school with the corrected report and did so with my tail between my legs.

For the most part, things went smoothly. Lila, my boss, was generous with her yearly evaluations and as long as she had no negative feedback from principals, and I followed proper paperwork procedures, I was free to run my programs as I saw fit. Lila observed me twice a year and I had to submit yearly goals, which were easily met. Lila did mention that one principal complained to her that I was working with too few students, was overpaid, and only practiced ball skills with one student in particular. I met with him and explained that the student's goals and objectives were about ball skills, *and* he had signed the IEP. Checkmate!

CHAPTER 14

ADAPTED PE THE END GAME

The years seemed to fly by and before I knew it, I had been teaching Adapted PE for fifteen years. One day I demonstrated a forward roll for some of my more advance students. When I popped up, the world was spinning. Maybe I was getting too old for forward rolls. When I entered a classroom to pick up a student, I was used to hearing, "Is that your father?" Then one day I heard a classmate whisper, "Who is that, your grandfather?" Ouch, that hurt.

I worked with a Roseville boy named Kyle who had Marfan's syndrome. As is usual with Marfan's, Kyle was very tall, had poor vision, and was uncoordinated. He stood close to six feet tall in the fifth grade. He was likable boy with a sharp sense of humor. Kyle loved basketball and it was a natural activity for him considering his height. Luckily, he was the only boy I worked with at his school and we had a gym to ourselves. One morning we were playing a modified game of basketball when I took a rebound away from Kyle. He looked at me incredulously shouting, "What are you, the Dennis Rodman of the geriatric crowd?" I was getting old and he knew it. Kyle became a star on the playground after he learned to shoot baskets. I watched him being chosen first for pickup games and felt comfortable dismissing him the following year.

As the years wore on, I noticed a disturbing trend. More and more children, especially boys, were being diagnosed with Autism Spectrum Disorder. Many of these were in regular classes and thus my caseload was growing. The majority of these boys had Asperger's syndrome, a higher functioning form of Autism. I was once told the "Autistic children don't live in our world, Asperger children do but don't play by our rules." In my experience this was so true. Autism has a bell shaped curve as I learned in Oakland. Most of my APE autistic students were on the high functioning end of that curve, but not all. One boy in Penryn was on the lower end, reminding me of my Judy in Oakland. He was a tall boy who continually twirled and shook his hands, never gave eye contact, and did not speak. I was unable to get him interested in any objects, balls, bean bags, hula hoops, or even the parachute, usually a sure thing. We were only able to work on balance, and basic movement activities such as running beside me or standing on one leg. I applaud the staff at Penryn for making adjustments for this boy. He must have been difficult to handle in a regular third grade class.

On the other end of the equation, was Jimmy an eleven-year-old boy in Foresthill Middle School with Asperger's. He was the pest of the school. Always in trouble for his language, fighting, and leaving the classroom without permission in a huff. At the same time he was intelligent, understood his differences, and could be very likable one-on-one. I had no trouble getting him out of his classroom. Teachers were more than happy to see him gone. Jimmy and I had the whole gym available to ourselves as well as the track and playground. I found Jimmy's view of the world fascinating. "They don't like me here, but I like a lot of them," he would shout to me. If something was on his mind, it would exit his mouth. "I want to shoot that bastard, Zack," he would snort with anger.

"Why?" I asked.

"Well, one day he looked at Monica funny," was his reply.

"A little over the edge for a funny look. Don't you think?" I gave back to him.

"Well maybe not shoot him then, but punch him a bit," he replied.

"Better, I guess," I thought. Was that progress? Jimmy and I ran on the track, and he worked up to a mile by the end of our year together. It seemed to take some of the angst out of our boy. Years later, I met Jimmy in a coffee shop when his sheltered workshop group was visiting. "Hey, you're Mr. T, you used to make me run and I still do." Little rewards from former students in APE are few and far between but very gratifying when they occur.

Another Asperger student was Bobby. He was a slightly built third grader with a curious grin emanating through his buck teeth. He, like Jimmy, said whatever thought passed through his head. Unlike Jimmy, he was not an angry child, just confused. I worked with him and three other students, but he took eighty percent of my time. "Why are we doing catching again?" he would ask. "This is stupid," came another proclamation. While running to catch a spinning hula hoop, he came to me in a panic. "Mr. T, I think my heart is beeping."

"That is a good thing, Bobby, it means you are alive and exercising," I said. He then would consistently check to see if his heart was "beeping." If he couldn't feel it, another panic would set in. His poor mother now had to deal with a beeping heart as well as Bobby's other daily quirks.

As often as I was assigned the student who drove the entire staff to distraction from the principal to the custodian, I sometimes had students who provided inspiration and pride in their schools. One such student was a small third grade girl from Lincoln. Monica was a sweet natured Hispanic girl with sparkling eyes, a wry smile, and a gentle disposition. She was born with a congenital abnormality affecting her arms and hands. The arms were inverted and fused. She was not able to grasp with her hands as her palms were facing outward with thumbs down. Monica let none of this stop her from fully participating with her class in all activities. She learned to catch a ball with her arms, to throw with a modified chest pass, and she could kick with the best of them. She loved to be physically fit and she could out run most of the boys. I never saw Monica without a smile and there was never an "I can't do that" moment. I met her parents only once. They used Spanish as a first language, but encouraged Monica to speak English. They never held their daughter back in any way and their pride in Monica was more than apparent.

Most parents were understanding, cooperative, and wanting only the best for their child. Most saw Special Education teachers as partners in meeting their child's needs. However, this was not always the case. I recall an IEP meeting with a multitude of professionals attending. The parents of an autistic child felt the County Office of Education was not meeting all of their demands. They brought a lawyer to the meeting who demanded all the possible services available for their boy. This two hour meeting was heated, very emotionally charged, and was adjourned without an agreement. I didn't attend the next session, but I understand that it lasted another two hours before some agreement was hammered out. Another IEP brought together two parents who were recently divorced and bitterness was filling the air. Each wanted to claim ownership of their child's education. It was apparent to all others attending that a counselor was needed, not for the student, but for the parents. It wasn't just his physical disability that was a deterrent, the poor boy was emotionally a mess.

I support the idea of the Least Restrictive Environment as defined by PL 94-142, but occasionally it is miss used. Some parents insist on placing their special needs child in inappropriate classes. A friend of mine had a son who was a low functioning Down boy. Teddy attended kindergarten with his peers and successfully completed the year with the help of a full time aide and numerous special help including, language therapy, occupational therapy, *and* adapted PE. By first grade, Teddy had become a major behavior problem. He would refuse a task, by falling to the floor in a defiant posture. He became the class "mascot" to the girls in his room, while the boys ignored or teased him. As academics became more important, Teddy's behavior problems escalated, he became more of a frustration to his classroom teachers. Teddy was not receiving the help he really needed. I saw him once a week for the first three years of his schooling. At IEP meetings, I bit my lip. My job was not about placement of a student in anything but my program. Finally, and reluctantly,

Teddy's parents agreed to place him in a special class in a different school. The change in Teddy was remarkable. He was in a class that was designed to meet his unique needs. He could still be with "normal" children during music, recess, lunch, and assemblies, but was getting the special training and skills that were necessary. I saw Teddy occasionally in his new school. He was a happy, well-adjusted child. From my experience the best solution to the Least Restrictive Environment clause for many pupils is having special classes in regular schools. The children can then be included in regular classrooms as little or as much as is appropriate for their well-being. Resources classrooms often fit this criteria.

I was asked to include a middle school child in my growing caseload. He was fully included only because of the parent's insistence. I was alarmed to see the condition of my new student. He was confined to a wheelchair, which was not the problem. He seemed severely impaired, had no language, no body control, and would not even give eye contact. He had a full-time aide who wiped his drool, fed, and toileted him. I was unable to do anything for him other than waste my valuable time trying to help him. During the year's annual IEP, his mother insisted that her son was improving. He was not! His poor mother was delusional. Unfortunately, the middle school was only a repository for him. Teachers drew straws to see who would have to endure having him in their classes.

I worked in a small k-8 school in the tiny foothill town of Dutch Flat. It was a long drive, but I enjoyed being among the tall pines, cool mountain air, and supportive staff. One boy who I saw weekly was an intelligent sixth grader with severe arthritis. Although he was a good athlete, he was often excluded from physical activities. I supervised his range of motion, strength exercises, and monitored his weekly progress or regression. I was conflicted with his program because it boarded on physical therapy and I felt that APE should not be considered physical therapy. In this case, I saw no alternative and stayed within the bounds of my specialty.

Another student at Dutch Flat was Amber, a legally blind fifth grader. Amber was a lovely and an utterly remarkable girl. Her sight had digressed over the last few years and she wore dark glasses at all times. Unlike our perceptions of the blind living in perpetual darkness, Amber could only see brilliant, glaring, and painful whiteness. I sometimes challenged my students to match me doing exercises, pull ups, arm extensions, or maybe sit-ups. I did this with Amber. I managed to do sixty crunches (modified sit-ups) in one minute. Amber surprised me by doing forty. A month later, she challenged *me*. I was shocked when she did seventy. I managed only sixty-five. She had been exercising at her home on a daily basis. Her aware parents bought her a treadmill and Amber would spend long winter months listening to music while running in her room. She and I did a five kilometer run together in the spring.

I continued to run about five times a week and to compete in running events. Suzi entered many one hundred mile events and was among the first women ever to run the four biggest hundred mile runs in one summer, the Grand Slam. To cap that off, she did a fifth. Not to be completely outdone, I entered a total of fourteen such weekend long events over the years, finishing eleven, and managed to finish a total of seventy-five ultras. They were always difficult. As I once said, "If you start to feel good during an ultra, don't worry you will get over it." It was fun to run in such diverse places as Vermont, British Columbia, Wisconsin, Colorado, Los Angles, and Utah. I usually saw familiar faces at these trail tests of athletic endurance. It was once said the most important trait for an ultrarunner is a bad memory. I never won an ultra, but did manage a few overall victories in shorter races.

Suzi and I became good friends with a couple in Hawaii and were able to visit the islands often during my spring break. Our friends, John and PJ, were ultrarunners and headed a running club called, with tongue in cheek, HURT (Hawaiian Ultra Running Team). With their help we did adventure runs on Maui, the Big Island, Molokai, Kauai, as well as fun runs on Oahu. It was wonderful to return to Hawaii after so many years. I drove to Nanakuli and found the shack I once lived in. I may have been the last person to have lived there. The roof was gone and the walls were covered in vines.

One day I was challenged by John, the HURT president, to run a new trail near his Oahu home without stopping. I took up his dare. I sloshed through mud, over slick rocks, and around rotting guava. I was drenched with sweat, covered with mud, and finished looking like a modern version of the tar-baby. I ended in a parking lot on top of the Pali, a well-known tourist attraction. There must have been four busloads of Japanese tourist all armed with Nikons snapping pictures of this strange mud covered, gray-haired American, gasping for breath while wearing skimpy shorts. What were they thinking? What was I thinking!

One spring break we passed on Hawaii and instead joined John and PJ on a cruise to Tahiti. Suzi and I had scuba cards, so we spent a lot of time in deep water. To this day I think Bora Bora is the most beautiful island anchored in the deep blue and, by the way, the most expensive.

I found that the years of running were beginning to take their toll on my body, particularly on my back. I lost my smooth stride and felt a constant hamstring pull. It was diagnosed as sciatica, but I persevered and joined the walking or running wounded in ultras. As a friend once said, an ultra-quiz we play is "what's my lesion." I often felt the back tighten on me during my PE sessions, especially with any twisting motions. Hockey was particularly annoying. Because of this, I was contemplating returning to the classroom for the last few years of my teaching.

I had a box full of medals, ribbons, and trophies from my competitions. They were just collecting dust, so I decided to put them to good use. I would reward my students for performances above and beyond expectations. Certainly Amber got one for her sit-ups and completing a five kilometer run. When a student met all goals and was dismissed from the program he or she was given a trophy. I think the rewards acted as motivation to those students who were not recipients. I know I enjoyed the looks on the faces of my students winning rewards that only the school athletes usually receive.

I worked with a seventh grader from Dutch Flat named Donny. He had Spina Bifida, and had been walking with the support of crutches. However, he often developed open sores on his feet because he had no sensations of pain. These lesions easily became infected. His concerned parents used a salve on his feet and while Donny slept one night, his dog, smelling the lotion, chewed his toes. He lost several of them, and spent his seventh grade year in a wheelchair. In spite of his setback, Donny was a joy to work with. He had the usual twelve year old sense of sarcastic humor which was often at my expense. One morning in the late fall, Donny asked about my belt buckle. I was wearing one I had earned at the Vermont 100. He said, "It says one hundred miles in one day. Did you drive?" he smirked.

"No way," I said, "it was a running race on trails."

"You mean an old fart like you can run one hundred miles?" Donny asked with a sly smile. "If you can do that then I can."

"Okay," I replied, "you're on."

Donny and I marked a running track on the playground of one tenth of a mile. "Ten times around equals one mile. That means you'll have to do one thousand laps. Are you up for that?" I asked. Donny said he could do it and accepted the challenge. His parents and his teacher liked the idea. So Donny began his epic journey. His classmates were very supportive as was the entire staff at Dutch Flat. Each day when his class was at PE Donny would wheel around the set track. He had a chart in the room measuring his progress. When I saw him weekly we would review his progress. He started slowly doing only a mile or two a week, but soon he gained strength and endurance and his pace increased. An added benefit was a substantial weigh loss. I belonged to an ultrarunning newsgroup and posted about Donny's run. Soon runners from around the country were sending Donny email letters of encouragement. He even got letters from England and Australia. I printed the letters and Donny's teacher would read them to the class. Donny became a VIP in his school. He struggled with his goal. Dutch Flat has significant snow and then mud, but Donny achieved his one thousandth lap in late February.

A friend of mine from Victoria, British Columbia was so inspired by this story that he made a solid silver belt buckle for Donny, engraved with his name and finishing date. I was an assistant at the biggest trail fifty kilometer event in the country, known as the Cool Canyon Crawl. I invited Donny and his family to attend and had Donny as the official starter. Before the race Donny, his parents, and about one hundred runners "ran" a mile with Donny. He wearing his new one hundred mile belt buckle. It was a proud day for Donny, his family, and me. Donny's feet eventually healed, and he was able to get around on crutches. Six years later, I saw Donny working as a mechanic in a local garage. He seemed happy with his situation and fondly recalled his "run."

As Placer County continued to grow new schools were added and Pam and I were being overextended even more. Lila retired and we had a new Superintendent of Special

Services, named Larry Moses. His wife had been an Adapted PE Teacher so he was especially sensitive to our needs. Soon a third APE Specialist was hired. Mike joined us right out of college. He was a raw recruit, but was full of enthusiasm and fresh ideas. He worked with some high schools and also was sent back up to the Truckee-Lake Tahoe schools. He took students cross country skiing and horseback riding, while Pam took some of our students to her husband's new rope course. APE was taking off in a good way in Placer County.

In the spring of 1997, I entered a fifty kilometer race in the Bay Area called the Olohne Wilderness Trail Run. The previous year I had won the fifty year age group. Winning my age group in an ultra was a first for me. When I looked at the entry list, I noticed that famed photographer and adventurer Galen Rowell was in the race. He had won the age group in 1996. I don't have heroes, but Galen was someone who I considered a great Renaissance man and I looked up to him. I introduced myself to him at the start and he, in turn, introduced me to his friend Conrad Anker. At the time Conrad was among the elite mountain climbers in the world. I was awed to be in their presence. I saw Galen fly by me at the top on the first climb and assumed that I would not see him until the finish. Conrad and I chatted on the next major ascent and I offered him some electrolyte tablets I carried. He later told me they saved his day. As I entered the last of five aid stations, there was Galen. I scampered through without him seeing me and ran like hell downhill to the finish. I won the age group by a little under a minute. Galen, Conrad, and I soaked tired feet and limbs in a nearby lake and shared a ride back to the start. In this time and place I was an equal with these two men whom I greatly admired.

Years later, I was scheduled to take a photography workshop of Galen's, when the terrible news hit the Internet that, "Famed photographer Galen Rowell and his wife Barbara were killed today in a single engine plane crash in Bishop California." I was devastated and felt I had lost a friend.

In the summer of the same year, I entered the Hardrock 100 mile run in Colorado. It has a reputation as the most difficult trail run in the country. The low point was over seven thousand feet and one of the eleven climbs was over fourteen thousand. It was not my day. My lungs filled with fluid, and I was forced to withdraw at just over fifty miles. Suzi did finish just under the time limit. It was her fourth try. I was happy for her but felt unfulfilled with my effort. Times were tough in our household that summer as we each withdrew to our offices. I need closure and so I signed up for the Eagle 100 in British Columbia in spite of my consistent sciatica.

Suzi and I were invited to a three day ninety-three mile run on the Wonderland Trail which circumnavigated Mount Rainier in Washington State. Twenty three runners had a support crew who hauled our gear between campsites and cooked wonderful dinners. I ran well, often running with a group from the Vancouver BC area. By the time the three days were over, most of the participants knew that Suzi and I would soon end our ten year relationship. Unfortunately I was left out of the loop, but knew the relationship was collapsing. A few weeks later, I completed my final one hundred at "the Eagle," which finished at a ski area above the

Okanagan Valley in British Columbia. Deborah Askew volunteered to be my pacer and she was a delight. We had run much of the Wonderland Trail together, so Deborah knew of my impending separation. Within a week so did I.

Suzi had met someone who fulfilled her dream more than I ever did or could. I was shocked. In hindsight, I should have seen it on the horizon. It was a difficult way to begin a new school year with little direction and little sleep. I once fell asleep in my car waiting for the lunch recess to finish when a knock on the window awakened me. It was the school principal following up on a lead of "a strange man sleeping in his car near the playground." My heart was not in my teaching that fall, but then working with the kids took me away from my own trauma, if only for a few hours. Suzi was off to Australia with her significant other and I had some time to breathe and reflect. Deborah and I wrote daily emails and I found that I had the support of many friends. It was these things that got me through the tough times. My colleague, Pam, was a great help with her homespun wisdom. Slowly I put things into perspective. Having Suzi move on was better than having an unhappy relationship. Divorcing even once in my family was seen as failure, but twice was beyond belief. My sisters and mother, however, were supportive.

Deborah visited me in California and we agreed to meet once more to run Rim to Rim to Rim in the Grand Canyon, forty-four miles and over ten thousand feet of vertical. It was our first real running date, I should have seen what was in store for me. We met about once a month in either California, Vancouver B.C. (her home), or occasionally somewhere in between. It soon became apparent that we wanted to be together more than once a month. Crossing the border so often was an unwelcome activity by US Immigration. So during Christmas Vacation in 1996 at Perkins Cove in Maine we decided apply for a fiancé visa. Deb moved to Weimar that summer and we were married one year after the day we met.

Deborah made a point of joining me at my job. She was shocked when I told a fourth grade girl that, "Girls can't play sports." It was tongue in cheek, of course. My girls would usually argue with me which was, the desired response. At this stage in my teaching career, I was looking forward to retirement and was planning on doing so when I turned sixty. Deb with her accounting background said, "Let's crunch the numbers." We did and my expected retirement date was shortened significantly. I had three peers die in one year's time. All were educators in their early fifties. Much too young and a warning to me that time is short. Deb and I had a shared love of travel. We visited Bali on our first overseas trip and this kindled that love of adventure. While teaching, travel was restricted to school vacations when prices were high and venues crowded. Retirement meant traveling when *we* wanted not when the school calendar dictated.

With the turn of the century came an unexpected enhancement to my retirement projection. Our county teacher negotiating team felt the time was right to ask for more compensation which had not been adjusted for several years. I, along with two others, was asked to present our proposal to the school board in a public forum. Because I worked in so many schools, I was able to stress that other districts had offered more to their staffs than our county office had. To our surprise the board listened and we were offered the best package in over ten years, a sizable increase in salary *and* a bonus for a master's degree—a long sought after benefit. Meanwhile the California State Teacher's Retirement System (CALSTRS), in order to reward teacher's for longevity, added bonuses for thirty, thirty-one, and thirty-two years in the system. They would base final compensation on only the highest salary year as opposed to taking an average of the highest three years, but only for teachers with over twenty years of service. Then our retiring governor, Pete Wilson, offered a ten percent increase to school districts, a real surprise because he had gone to battle with teachers throughout his tenure. When we put the numbers on paper, I would receive a twenty-eight percent increase in my retirement compensation. Wow! Deborah decided that I could retire in 2002. Because I began teaching in Oakland and thus the CALSTRS system in January, if I could convince my supervisor that a half-year contract was to his benefit, I would be able to leave my position in January.

Larry Moses was at first reluctant to give me the January date for retirement. I then pointed out that many colleges graduate students at the end of the fall term, I could work with my replacement to ease he or she into the routine, and God knows a new replacement would work for less than half the salary I was drawing. I think the last point hit the mark and I signed a contract for half the year. I felt relieved, to say the least.

The last year I worked in twenty-three schools every week, had more and longer lasting IEP's, and now had to update student's goals twice a year. The paper avalanche was becoming overwhelming, leaving less time to actually teach. The job really wasn't being done adequately under these conditions.

September 2011 was the beginning of my last year. One Friday morning, I was preparing for work while watching the Today Show, when the first plane struck the World Trade Center. I watched in horror as the second plane struck and the towers fell. I went to work dazed by the events in New York and knew the world was changing. My first group that day was at EV Cain Middle School in Auburn. One of my students was very animated and excited. He seemed to have enjoyed the attack. He was an Asperger's boy and was not in touch with the reality of the situation. I actually had to break up a fight between him and another student. That was a first in my APE career.

The next Friday we had a workshop with about thirty Northern California APE teachers. We had a moment of silence and then sang "GOD BLESS AMERICA." For the first time after the monstrous events of the previous week, I lost it. Tears flooded down my cheeks as Mike put his arm around me in sympathy. That year seemed to drag on. I made sure to update all of my files, inform all the students and teachers that change was coming, and prepared for a smooth transition. In November, Larry and I interviewed three candidates for my replacement after doing a paper screening of all applicants. We chose a young woman and recent college graduate named Carrie. She was bright eyed and ready to go. She had been substitute teaching and was thrilled to have her ideal job as an Adapted PE Specialist. I only hoped that she was up to the task.

That winter Deborah and I planned a trip to Belize in February as a retirement celebration. I was still concerned about finances, but we had paid off the mortgage thanks to Deborah's funds, so retirement seemed very workable. I filed the papers with CALSTRS and we were committed. The first two weeks in January, Carrie and I spent together. She was introduced to my (now her) children, teachers, and administrators. After school we reviewed files, IEPs, and County procedures. I encouraged her lead some of the sessions with students and tried not to interfere, although the kids kept looking toward me for direction. The next week was my last. Carrie spent part of the week with Pam to see how she handled the work load. Thursday and Friday Carrie was on her own as I worked in my office cleaning out twenty-six years of memories, most positive, but some trying. That week Pam had a farewell dinner for me at her house. It included Deb and I, Pam and her husband, Mike, Carrie, my two supervisors Larry and Lila, and David and Larry, the APE teachers from neighboring Nevada County. The following week there was another retirement dinner at a local restaurant where I said goodbye to county staff. I was pleased to have Chris F. present. He was among my very first students and now he was a successful young man.

And so I closed the teaching chapter of my life. I would not change it if I had to start again, the Camp Wediko boys, the Hawaiian girls in their colored dresses and flowers in their hair, the shiny faced fifth graders in New Hampshire, the troubled clients on Napa's B ward, the rough minority students on one Oakland's toughest streets, the first autistic class in Oakland, the Special Ed. classes in peaceful Placer County, and lastly, the twenty years as an APE Specialist. I walked out that day with a sense of satisfaction, not of a job well done, but of the effort I had put in. It was another ultra of sorts and I had crossed the finish line.

EPILOGUE

It has been twelve years since I left the Placer County Office of Education and my work as an Adapted PE Specialist. I initially thought I would enjoy working part-time as a substitute teacher for the PCOE. I applied and was turned down because I did not file proper reference papers with my application. This, after working for them for twenty-six years. I know it was just a secretarial SNAFU, but I was not pleased and did not continue the application process. Within two months, my boss, Larry, contacted me asking me to work because my replacement Carrie was pregnant. By that time, I had become more than happy with my retirement schedule and I turned him down.

Deborah continued work as an accountant for her Canadian firm, usually from our home, but also traveling to Vancouver to meet personally with her clients. Her April was spent working twelve hour days in Vancouver preparing taxes. I often joined her there. Vancouver became our second home, and we still have many friends in this northern city of water and glass. The back woes became too much and I reluctantly gave up running. I began cycling four of five times a week using both my road and mountain bikes and would hike on my familiar trails.

The STRS retirement checks began to roll in and we gratefully used them to fulfill our passion for travel. Trips to Belize and Bali were followed by cruises on small ships in the Caribbean. Deb's dad and stepmother lived in Portugal and we visited with them several times. We hiked some great trails, including the Haute Route in France and Switzerland, the Inca Trail in Peru, the Milford Track in New Zealand, and the trail to Everest Basecamp in Nepal.

Life moves on and so did we. I was tired of caring for our two-and-one-half acres of forest and knew that the California property was overvalued. We decided to put it on the market and sold just before the 2006 housing crash. With the new funds we were able to move to the lovely Heber Valley I had first seen so long ago. Both Deb and I had finished the Wasatch Front 100. It ended in the charming Wasatch Mountain town of Midway and there we made our home. Life was good there. Deb was able to retire, I took up golf (still playing poorly), skiing (I ski as bad as I golf), and did more cycling (at least I can ride my bike well). Deb continued to run and cross-county ski. However, we found winters more and more challenging, so we purchased a small second home in the red rock country of Saint George, Utah. Eventually we moved there full time. We enjoy the hiking trails and the warm weather. At this writing we have traveled to all seven continents and to over one hundred countries and are still long for more. (Another book?) Life is good.

One of the downsides to Special Education teaching has been the lack of feedback from former students. I worked with. For the most part they are incapable of writing to thank teachers for a job well done. I was only a small part of their school life as an APE teacher, but I can only hope I had a significant influence. My children in Hawaii, New Hampshire, and Oakland are now all middle-aged adults and hopefully coping with their own lives successfully. I found out recently that Henry "Buzz" Glass died at the age of ninety-seven. His inspiration and enthusiasm for movement lives on in his many recordings and books.   Mine was a wonderful career, and I don't regret any of it. I am sure that I may have missed many significant stories and people in my accounts. I hope no one will feel left out or offended by shaky recall or omission.

ABOUT THE AUTHOR

Gene lives with his wife, Deborah, in Saint George, Utah. His daughter, Dawn, goes by the name Woniya and lives in Hood River, Oregon. Gene and Deborah still enjoy traveling exploring the canyon country of the Southwest. Gene's travel photos can be seen at gtbow.smugmug.com.

www.ingramcontent.com/pod-product-compliance
Lightning Source LLC
Chambersburg PA
CBHW060229050426
42448CB00009B/1358